Negotiating Strategically

Negotiating Strategically

One Versus All

Andreas Nikolopoulos

Professor of Conflict Management and Negotiations, Athens University of Economics and Business, Greece

Originally published in Greece in 2009 by Patakis Publishers as
Μόνος Εναντίον Όλων: Η Στρατηγική των Διαπραγματεύσεων
(Alone Against All: The Negotiation Strategy), ISBN 978–960–16–3306–0

First published 2011 by
PALGRAVE MACMILLAN

Palgrave Macmillan in the UK is an imprint of Macmillan Publishers Limited, registered in England, company number 785998, of Houndmills, Basingstoke, Hampshire RG21 6XS.

Palgrave Macmillan in the US is a division of St Martin's Press LLC, 175 Fifth Avenue, New York, NY 10010.

Palgrave Macmillan is the global academic imprint of the above companies and has companies and representatives throughout the world.

Palgrave® and Macmillan® are registered trademarks in the United States, the United Kingdom, Europe and other countries.

ISBN 978–0–230–29846–0

This book is printed on paper suitable for recycling and made from fully managed and sustained forest sources. Logging, pulping and manufacturing processes are expected to conform to the environmental regulations of the country of origin.

A catalogue record for this book is available from the British Library.

A catalog record for this book is available from the Library of Congress.

10   9   8   7   6   5   4   3   2   1
20   19   18   17   16   15   14   13   12   11

Printed and bound in Great Britain by
MPG Group, Bodmin and King's Lynn

To all of you who, despite your intentions, made me
mature in handling conflicts and negotiations

CONTENTS

List of Tables   ix

List of Figures   x

List of Case Studies   xi

List of Examples   xiii

Acknowledgments   xv

Preface   xvii

Chapter 1   **Introduction**   **1**
                 1.1 Why we negotiate and when   1

Chapter 2   **Conflict, power and negotiation**   **4**
                 2.1 Forms of direct negotiation   6
                 2.2 Virtual negotiation and isolated acts   6
                 2.3 Effective negotiations   7
                 2.4 Principles of a general model for
                      conflict handling   9
                 2.5 Stages of the conflict model   12
                 2.6 Summary   16

Chapter 3   **Forming initial behavior**   **17**
                 3.1 Possible desired behaviors   17
                 3.2 The three components of behavior   19
                 3.3 The structure of relationships   20
                 3.4 The cost of conflicts   27
                 3.5 Conflict ability   34
                 3.6 The desire to engage in conflicts   37
                 3.7 Summary   49
                 3.8 Moving on to the next stage   51

Chapter 4   **The power budget**   **53**
                 4.1 The components of relationship fields   55
                 4.2 Negotiating behaviors within the fields   56
                 4.3 The relationships between fields   56

	4.4 The cost of conflict within fields	61
	4.5 Conflict ability within fields	67
	4.6 Behavior formation within fields	70
	4.7 Summary	78
Chapter 5	**Conditions and efficiency**	**84**
	5.1 The sources of efficiency	84
	5.2 Types and content of conditions	92
	5.3 Conditions: characterization and measurements	109
	5.4 Efficiency: preservation and improvement	113
	5.5 Summary	119
	5.6 Moving on to the next stage	121
Chapter 6	**Evaluation of consequences**	**122**
	6.1 The process of selecting conflict-handling strategies	124
	6.2 Criteria for determining the consequences	125
	6.3 Using criteria for the determination of consequences	132
	6.4 Summary	141
Chapter 7	**Ways to handle a conflict**	**143**
	7.1 "Win" and "lose" concepts in negotiations	144
	7.2 Direct negotiations	146
	7.3 Virtual negotiations	162
	7.4 Isolated actions	170
	7.5 Summary so far	172
	7.6 Before the final decision	173
	7.7 Reaching the end	179
	7.8 Final remarks	180
Chapter 8	**Epilog**	**182**
Index		187

LIST OF TABLES

3.1	Estimation of Helen's cost of conflict	30
4.1	Conflict cost and field significance combinations	66
5.1	William, Paul and Cargo's deficits	93
5.2	John's and Chris's political data	95
5.3	Timing data in Tom's and Bill's negotiation	98
5.4	The cultural conditions during Ellie's negotiation with Alex	101
5.5	Legal conditions in Paul's and Cristina's conflict	103
5.6	The course of negotiations between Mark and Brian	105
5.7	Joan's unfavorable complementary conditions	107
5.8	Obstacles to A's and B's efficiency	112
7.1	The interests of the parties regarding the street market	152
7.2	Georgia's and Anna's negotiation	157
7.3	Combined negotiating strategies among the parties	174

LIST OF FIGURES

1.1 Subjective and objective obstacles by goal realization   3
3.1 Behavior's components for desired conflict behaviors   20
3.2 The controversial elements in a relationship   24
3.3 Measuring the conflict in a relationship   28
3.4 The relationships between behavior components   38
3.5 Combinations of components and conflicting behavior   50
3.6 Path to the power budget   51
4.1 Components of fields and negotiating behaviors   57
4.2 Relationships with players in other fields   57
4.3 The fields of relationships in case study 4.3(a)   59
4.4 The possible combinations between fields   71
4.5 Behaviors within fields   79
4.6 The transition to the stage of conditions   83
5.1 Power quantity and efficiency   87
5.2 Adapting to the other party's data   90
5.3 Transition to the stage of the consequences   120
6.1 The conflict handling selection process   125
6.2 Seeking the sources of the consequences   134
7.1 Ways to handle a conflict   143
7.2 Interest-based and positional bargaining   148
7.3 Influencing process of negotiating data   167
7.4 Interaction points between A and B's behavior   177
7.5 The course and end of the conflict episode   179

LIST OF CASE STUDIES

1.1   Should Kevin stay with Star or resign?   1
1.2   Anna's promotion is at risk   2
2.1   Alex's parallel conflicts   10
3.1   Catherine's work life burden   21
3.2   Helen's conflict and cooperation   29
3.3   Power distribution   35
3.4   The aggravated general manager   37
3.5   Irene chooses depreciation to gain future benefits   39
3.6   Ted's depreciation choice   40
3.7   Holly and her new job   41
3.8   Phil is interested in the new client   42
3.9   Two seminar speakers face an incompatible behavior   44
3.10 Alexa's attempt to depreciate is misunderstood   47
3.11 Is Jacob going to overshadow Charlie?   48
3.12 Eventually, will Paul become a businessman?   49
4.1   Elisabeth finds herself in a reaction dilemma   54
4.2   Carl is changing his promotion plans   54
4.3   Dan, his wife and supplier X   58
4.4   Rose and her workload   61
4.5   Zoë questions her conflict ability   68
4.6   Theo's unacceptable workload   69
4.7   Eve depreciates her conflicts   72
4.8   Fred and his tough client   74
4.9   Penelope fights against the public sector   75
4.10 Sean risks exposure   76
4.11 Lea must wait   78
4.12 Cristina is enmeshed in inflexible fields   80
4.13 Chris chooses his symbolic action   81
4.14 Adam wants to be hired at X Company   82
5.1   Peter is discredited   85
5.2   Jessica and the purchase of Carl's apartment   89
5.3   William is performing audits for Cargo   92
5.4   John and Chris are involved in a long-lasting conflict   94

5.5	Tom's and Bill's time conditions	98
5.6	Ellie and Alex's cultural profile	100
5.7	Paul and his lawyer threaten Cristina	102
5.8	Mark, Brian and the special paint coating	104
5.9	Joan, Mary, and 70 purchase managers	106
6.1	Nick, his collaborators and the proposal to Jim	122
6.2	Katrina, her subordinates and Helen	131
6.3	Kevin manipulates the department and the management	137
7.1	Casino "Kings": Pit, Elinor and the mediator	149
7.2	Al, the Mayor and Harry	151
7.3	Peter negotiates with Vickie at the Blue Star Hotel	154
7.4	A large mobile phones deal: Georgia vs. Anna	156
7.5	Tina, Alice, and the merger of Chemicals S.A.	164
7.6	Jenny risks losing her job because of Fred	168
7.7	How Kate and Nick drifted apart	171

LIST OF EXAMPLES

2.1	The boomerang effect	8
3.1	Depreciated conflict	18
3.2	Conflict action	18
3.3	Conflict accumulation	19
3.4	Material conflicts and cooperations	23
3.5	Decreasing emotional conflicts	26
3.6	Expanding relationships	26
3.7	Emotional cooperation	27
3.8	Balancing deficits	33
5.1	Timing of a conflict	96
5.2	Unavoidable failure	96
5.3	Effects of unavoidable failure	97
5.4	Duration of power use	97
5.5	Relevant ancillary conditions	109
5.6	Irrelevant ancillary conditions	110
5.7	Exploiting the mix	111
5.8	Avoiding obstacles (1)	115
5.9	Avoiding obstacles (2)	116
5.10	Avoiding obstacles (3)	117
5.11	Expanding conditions	117
5.12	Shaping the mix of conditions	119
6.1	Cost and damages (1)	126
6.2	Costs and damages (2)	126
6.3	Costs and damages (3)	127
6.4	Costs and damages (4)	127
6.5	Profit	128
6.6	Negative and positive influences	129
6.7	Duration of influences	130
6.8	Using criteria to determine conditions	133
6.9	Sources of consequences: power reserves	135
6.10	Sources of consequences: formation of initial behavior	135
6.11	Sources of consequences: conditions	136

7.1	Direct and indirect negotiation	144
7.2	"Win" and "lose" concepts in negotiations	145
7.3	Interest-based bargaining	147
7.4	Collective resolution	148
7.5	Effective direct negotiation	159
7.6	Isolated actions	170
7.7	Negotiation behavior mix	173

Acknowledgments

The idea of this book hinges on my article entitled "Planning the Use of Power: An Episodic Model" published in the *International Journal of Conflict Management* in 1995. The reason why it took so long for the publication of this book was that I needed the necessary accumulation of experiences which ultimately led me to furthering my views to such a degree and manner that I could not have foreseen.

These experiences came about from three sources: The first were my activities as a Mediator and Arbitrator for the National Organization for Mediation and Arbitration. I handled over 200 cases in the field of labor – management relations. The second source of my experiences was my engagement as a consultant in conflict handling for business relations. And, finally, the third source was my teaching of postgraduates in my courses on 'Negotiations' for part-time executive students in the Athens University of Economics and Business. During these courses my students presented numerous examples from their conflicts and negotiations arising during their own personal and working lives.

For this reason I wish to thank my students and at the same time to underline that the cases I refer to in this book are purely fictitious though grounded in reality.

Last, but not least, I wish to thank Drs Ilias Kapoutsis and Demetris Pittaoulis and also PhD Candidate Ioannis Blatsos for their accurate reviews of the materials in the book. In particular, Ilias Kapoutsis's comments were taken on board in a way that substantially helped the structure of the chapters in the book.

ANDREAS NIKOLOPOULOS

PREFACE

Negotiations are part of our everyday life. Many times we wished we had achieved more from a negotiation than we actually did, or were forced to behave in a way different from what we actually did.

There are two reasons for this shortcoming. The first reason is that, as a rule, we are burdened at the same time with different and not necessarily related issues arising from our work, family, personal relations, community, and so on. The second reason is that we have limited resources available to us when it comes to facing them in the best possible way, for example we have limited money, time, we have to consider possible trade-offs, rewards, promises, coercions, supports and the like.

The above two reasons keep us from claiming the greatest possible benefit from a specific relationship. This, we fear, would further decrease our resources so we might not be able to claim benefits from the rest of the relationships available to us. As a result and out of necessity we are led to pursuing *the greatest possible benefit from the total sum of our relations* instead of pursuing a single, isolated, one.

Thus, we need to come to an understanding that in order for us to hit these targets successfully we cannot be helped by a single specific way of negotiating in all cases. Instead, we choose that particular way which fits the specific case and which will lead us to the best possible outcome.

Each and every one of us is entirely alone at the center of each set of negotiations. In other words, individuals are alone versus all those who behave in a way which limits or endangers our benefits. The safeguarding of these benefits, that is to say the accomplishment of our aims, depends on the success of our handling of negotiations.

This book aims to cover 'negotiating strategically' and for this purpose we rely on the way of thinking that is used by all of us during negotiations. We are not going to dictate to the reader what should be done, but on the contrary we intend to identify with him or her, to adjust to the course of his/her way of thinking as to how best they are to overcome particular problems and survive in the best possible way being caught at the very center of the negotiations experienced.

I hope that in this book the reader will see him/her self through the examples and observations and thus will be able to judge their own behavior. Putting it differently, they will confirm those areas in which their negotiating strategy could be improved, which in itself is the core theme of this book.

ANDREAS NIKOLOPOULOS

CHAPTER 1

Introduction

1.1 Why we negotiate and when

If we ask the question "Why do we negotiate?", we are likely to receive a variety of answers: because of obligation, because we need to survive, to defend our benefits, because of our psychological needs, and many others. Regardless of the answer to the question, negotiation exists in our everyday lives and in all our relationships.

This happens because, in each of our relationships, the aim is the preservation or the expansion of our benefits. In achieving these goals we often have to face obstacles that lead to undesirable results. For this reason, every time these obstacles appear, we face the question of to how to deal with them. Obstacles fall into two categories: objective (case study 1.1) and subjective (case study 1.2).

The new development worries Kevin:

(a) He wants to move to a new company in order to have a larger salary.
(b) He has discovered that the company he wants to move to is negotiating its acquisition by another company.

Case study 1.1 Should Kevin stay with Star or resign?

1. Kevin has worked at Star for five years.
2. One of Star's competitors, Omega, offers him employment with a salary increased by 20% and with opportunities for rapid career progression.
3. Since this offer is attractive to Kevin, he is willing to discuss the employment details (e.g. the job description, his position within the company's hierarchy, and the number of subordinates).
4. Just before signing his contract with Omega, and prior to tendering his resignation to Star, Kevin discovers that Omega is negotiating its acquisition by another company, Kappa.

The new information causes Kevin concern since he has also been told that the employees' salaries at Kappa are lower than those paid by Omega. This means that, if Kappa buys out Omega, the salaries of the employees at Omega will be negatively affected. Furthermore, it will endanger Kevin's job and job description since everything will be restructured, bringing unexpected developments for the future of Omega employees.

On the basis of this information, Kevin is very skeptical about moving to Omega and so revises his plans for leaving Star.

These obstacles are objective obstacles and, therefore, not negotiable. In other words:

(a) Kevin cannot change Omega's plans regarding being bought out by Kappa; and
(b) Kevin would have no influence on how the incoming Kappa administration would deal with him.

Such obstacles force us either to revise our initial goals, or to seek new ways to achieve them, since these obstacles cannot be overcome in any other way.

Anna is facing a different type of problem than those in case study 1.1. Anna's obstacles are not objective; they are subjective, since they are caused by the *interests of other people*. Thus, Anna can deal with her

Case study 1.2   Anna's promotion is at risk

1. Anna works in a department with 15 people.
2. In this department there is an opportunity for promotion that Anna is trying to earn, so she can improve her salary and working conditions.
3. When Anna's ambitions regarding the promotion become evident, five of her colleagues place obstacles in her path for various reasons:
   (a) One is seeking the promotion for himself; if Anna were promoted, he would have to wait a further two years at least for the next promotion opportunity.
   (b) Two do not want Anna to be promoted because they believe that, as a manager, she will be especially demanding and they will have to work harder.
   (c) The remaining two colleagues want the other candidate to be promoted because they believe that they will benefit from him being the manager.

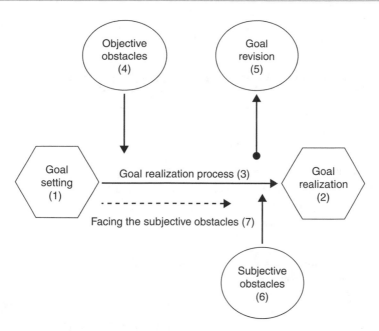

Figure 1.1   Subjective and objective obstacles by goal realization

obstacles differently than Kevin, since Anna can "safeguard" her goal by shaping the interests of her colleagues in such a way that they stop posing obstacles. If, alternatively, Anna adopted Kevin's approach, she would then have to face unacceptable losses and she would change her plans, forgetting the promotion. Figure 1.1 presents the distinction between objective and subjective obstacles in the process of goal realization.

According to Figure 1.1, we set goals (1) to be realized (2); en route to their realization (3), two types of obstacles present themselves. The first type of obstacle is objective (4) and its existence leads us to revise our goals (5). The second type of obstacle is subjective (6), since these obstacles are created by another party. These obstacles can be faced by changing the party's behavior, which has a reactive affect on the realization of our initial goals. Otherwise, we would be obliged to revise our initial goals, which would lead to corresponding losses.

CHAPTER 2

Conflict, power and negotiation

Negotiations presuppose a conflict of interest, together with an attempt to alter the other side's behavior through the use of power reserves: thus, conflict, negotiations and power are directly bound to each other. First, we discuss three basic negotiating strategies:

- Direct negotiations.
- Virtual negotiations.
- Isolated acts.

We then go on to introduce a new way of thinking and handling conflicts, based on the principles that each party:

- Possesses limited power reserves, and thus considers how to use them in an effective way.
- Experiences parallel conflicts in multiple contexts, and thus their behavior in a given conflict field can be explained by their activities and their committed power reserves in the remaining fields.
- Plans before acting, so that their negotiating methods follow a strategic rationale.

Considering case study 1.2, we see that Anna's five colleagues have a variety of reasons for their response to her plans for promotion. However, all of these reasons have a common foundation: if Anna accomplishes her goal, then the prospect of her colleagues is that each of them will experience a shortfall in achieving their personal goals:

- One colleague will be delayed in achieving his promotion.
- Two colleagues worry that their working conditions will become less conducive.
- The remaining two colleagues hope to improve their working conditions if their preferred candidate wins the promotion.

This shortfall is the presupposition of the existence of conflict; therefore:

A conflict arises when someone is not willing to accept the perceived deficit in his goals caused by the intrusion of others.

Differences of opinion – such as the most attractive color for a car, or which team will win the World Cup – do not adversely affect our goals; in other words, the preservation or earning of benefits.

When we acknowledge and do not accept the shortfall in our goals, we wish to eliminate it (i.e. we look for a way to handle our conflict). Obviously, the elimination of the shortfall in our goals depends on our ability to influence (i.e. change) the other party's behavior in such a way as to prevent it blocking the realization of our goals.

However, there has to be a reason for the other party's behavior to change. Of course, we may have experienced cases where the other party may unexpectedly change its behavior to our benefit, without our having made any efforts to achieve this. This may occur, for example, because there was an unexpected and drastic change in circumstances. Yet, it would be very risky to base our plans on such unexpected gifts. The plan for achieving the required change should be based on:

- The way the other party thinks.
- The way the other party acts.

Say, for example, I want to buy a specific house and the seller is asking an unreasonable price. I have two ways to bring the price down to an acceptable level. One way would be to prove to the seller that the price he is asking is too high, which leads to a "no way out situation"; or by giving some other benefit that is significant to but less significant to me (i.e. try to influence the seller's way of thinking, which would change his behavior).

Alternatively, I could warn him that I will harm his business relations with others if he does not agree to sell me the house at the price I wish to pay. In this way, I would try to influence the seller's behavior, regardless of his preferences.

Both these methods demand the use of certain means. These means are not difficult to determine, provided we think about what might change our own behavior: for example, information, impressions, excuses, pressures, rewards, promises, threats, support, control, prestige, knowledge, coercion, profits, exchanges, defamation, projection, misdirection. All of these means, and more, are included in the meaning of "power". For this reason:

> Power is any means that can be used for the change and control of another's behavior, with the aim of protecting one's own interests.

From this it can be inferred that the existence of conflict and the use of power are directly interconnected. This interconnection is based on the fact that successful conflict handling is possible only when we change the other party's behavior. This can occur through the use of means characterized as "power".

The most usual way power is used in social relationships is through the act of negotiation. For this reason:

> Negotiation is every interaction aimed at the safeguard of interests.

Since conflict precedes negotiation, the way people negotiate is based on the data emerging from the initial conflict.

2.1 Forms of direct negotiation

Direct (or "real") negotiation presupposes the natural presence of the parties and their efforts to cover their interests by the appropriate shaping of the other's behavior. In other words, there is direct negotiation if Anna (case study 1.2) meets with her four colleagues who were against her promotion, either individually or according to interest. During such meetings, in order to stop them responding negatively to her intention to be promoted she would try to change their opinions by means of relevant arguments and offers. She could reassure the two colleagues concerned about the demands she would make of them that they would have no cause for alarm if she were promoted; the other two colleagues could be reassured that their working conditions would promote their interests.

2.2 Virtual negotiation and isolated acts

Let us consider what would happen if Anna did not meet personally with her four colleagues but, rather, arranged a meeting between them and a neutral and trusted person. This person could present Anna's arguments and offers in order to stop the negative response to Anna's wish to be promoted.

This form of negotiation is "virtual", rather than "real": for various reasons, Anna chooses not to be present. However, her arguments and offers are presented in the way that Anna would have done had she participated in the meeting.

Would we have had negotiation if, due to their response to her possible promotion, Anna threatened her colleagues through a third person? The answer is "yes", since threats can also be expressed in direct negotiations.

Would we have negotiation, if Anna, instead of threatening her colleagues through a third person, arranged it so that one of them would be fired? The answer would be "no" for the person being fired, since the relationship with Anna is interrupted and no change of behavior is sought. Therefore, Anna's act towards him is an isolated act. However, by arranging for a member of staff to be fired, Anna expresses virtually what will happen to her other colleagues, should they persist in creating obstacles in her pursuit of promotion. In other words, Anna is reinforcing her message: "If you continue to go against my promotion, then you might be fired." Anna's act may also be virtual negotiation towards the colleague who is also seeking the promotion. This happens if Anna is willing to prove to him how powerful she is and, thus, prevent him from pursing the promotion Anna considers to be hers.

We can also characterize Anna's change in behavior towards the colleagues as virtual negotiation when the change in her general behavior is aimed at causing her colleagues concern, as though their negative impression of Anna were justifiable.

2.3 Effective negotiations

We often ask ourselves: How can we be effective in our negotiations?

Usually, this question is bound up with certain behaviors, such as whether:

- It is right or wrong to hide our interest in a certain benefit in order to avoid pressures from the other party on this point.
- It is right or wrong to be aggressive or difficult.
- It is right or wrong to include more people while negotiating.
- It is right or wrong to bluff.
- It is right or wrong to sit across from or next to the other party.
- It is right or wrong to cause feelings of insecurity in others.
- It is right or wrong to trust others.
- It is right or wrong to develop or emphasize our emotional relationships in negotiations.

- It is right or wrong to start with easy or pleasurable topics and then to progress to the hard or unpleasant topics.
- It is right to start the negotiation with "No".

People pose such questions because they experience inconsistent results from adopting such behaviors, and/or because they want to crosscheck the validity of advice from practitioners and scholars.

Experienced negotiators know how hard it is to answer such questions dogmatically. Our experience shows that there will be cases that cannot be answered. In other words, in every one of the suggested behaviors, there is no definitive "yes" or "no".

This is because there are no behaviors that are consistently right or wrong in every situation. The conduct of a negotiation depends on its compatibility with the elements of the conflict and of our relationship with the other party. In other words, it depends on the *model of conflict* that we are facing. Therefore, in some models of conflict, each of the behaviors described may be efficient or inefficient.

Any "recipes" that are recommended must be treated with caution. First, the "recipes" are probably inconsistent with the model of conflict to be resolved, and thus cannot lead us to the desired results. Second, the other party may be aware of our "recipes"; making us predictable and possibly neutralizing our efforts. In the worst case scenario, we may provoke the opposite of what we are seeking to achieve; in other words, we may be faced with a "boomerang effect" (Example 2.1).

In order to deal with problems like this, we must develop a system with which to evaluate our behaviors: in other words, a general conflict model that enables us to explain our own behavior in a conflict situation, thus making it easier for us to predict the other's negotiation behavior.

Before we summarize this general model, we will discuss its basic principles.

Example 2.1   The boomerang effect

A negotiations expert received a visit from an insurance agent who wanted to sell him life insurance. However, the agent's efforts failed: the negotiation expert became angry because he recognized the use of manipulative negotiation "recipes" that should be very familiar to any negotiation expert. In addition, he believed that the agent should have known that he was dealing with a negotiation expert who would be aware of such methods.

2.4 Principles of a general model for conflict handling

The general model for handling conflicts is based on the following three principles, according to which each of the involved parties:

- Principle 1: possesses limited power reserves.
- Principle 2: faces parallel conflicts in diverse relationships or conflict arenas.
- Principle 3: plans its action before acting, in other words they do not respond impulsively.

The degrees to which these principles are actually met confirm or diminish the validity of this model.

Principle 1: limited power reserves

It is very hard to find a type of power that would be inexhaustible or permanently available; for example, excuses, pressures, promises, threats, information, prestige, money, negative sanctions, and control.

The restriction of our power reserves in combination with their usefulness, since without them we cannot face conflicts, leads us to rationalize their use. In other words, limitations lead us to the avoidance of waste and inefficient use.

Principle 2: parallel conflicts

As a rule, when we face a conflict, seldom do we have the freedom to concentrate solely on that conflict, because we are facing parallel conflicts in other arenas. Examples of parallel conflicts are presented in case study 2.1.

Alex may not be so unlucky as to have to face all of these conflicts. As a rule, though, he will probably have to face more than one conflict at a time.

The principle of parallel conflicts, in combination with the principle of restriction of power reserves, means we have to decide how we are going to allocate our powers at the various levels of relationships in which we are involved.

With this distribution, we seek to achieve the best from the whole range of relationships in which we are involved, and not deal with each conflict

Case study 2.1   Alex's parallel conflicts

1. Alex's supervisor wants to avoid his personal responsibilities with regard to supplier problems and therefore accuses Alex.
2. Alex is asking his supervisor for permission to propose to the HR department that two of the 10 staff members be fired at the end of the week.
3. Alex is informed that one of his colleagues is speaking about him in a very derogatory way.
4. A very important customer is planning to place a large order with a competitor. If this happens, then some colleagues will seek to blame Alex for the company's loss.
5. A good customer asks Alex to accept a two-month deferral of payment for a debt of US$10,000.
6. The construction company that has taken on the renovation of Alex's house informs him of its intention to increase the price by US$5,000.
7. Alex's company is planning to suggest that he attend an educational program that will last one week and is 500 km away from his workplace. This will cause additional burdens on the family, his job and on his relationship with his supervisor, since his supervisor will think that Alex is seeking to prove himself of greater worth to the company than his supervisor.

in isolation. This naturally brings us to a forced compromise, since the ideal would be to take the maximum benefits from each level separately. That, however, will not be possible, since our power reserves are insufficient to obtain the maximum benefit from each conflict.

If Alex preferred not deal with all the conflicts facing him but, rather, those with the greatest priority, then his way of handling those conflicts would be different. However, if Alex had to face all these conflicts simultaneously, he would have to ignore some of them. In an effort to deal with all the conflicts, some matters would receive only superficial attention because he would not have the necessary power reserves to deal with all of them in the way he wished.

From this, therefore, we can conclude that:

- In order to have the conflict ability that we seek in a field of relationships, we need to devote sufficient power reserves for that purpose. If not, then we become inefficient.

- The power reserves that we use in a field of conflict are not necessarily what we would prefer but, rather, are those that allow us to allocate our power reserves in the rest of the fields in which we are active.
- The way we allocate our power reserves in all of our arenas shows the type of total benefits we are seeking, or think we can achieve.
- Even if one conflict seems to be unrelated to another, it is still connected indirectly since the power reserves we use for it are not available for other conflicts.
- The developments in one conflict influence our behaviors in our remaining arenas, since these developments increase or decrease the amount of power available for use in other arenas.
- If we do not take into consideration the limitations of our power reserves, then we are in danger of having our whole conflict ability collapse. This will happen because we will not be in a position to use sufficient power in the arenas that are vital to us due to the distribution of power reserves to less significant arenas or to arenas where we are inefficient.

Principle 3: plan before responding

The first principle of the limitation of power reserves shows the need for the rational use of our power reserves. This means that the use of our powers is conducted after planning, and not impulsively and spontaneously. The result of accepting this principle is that the object of negotiations falls into two stages: planning, and the realization of the negotiations.

Planning negotiations

This stage concentrates on the thoughts that come before the negotiation process, and therefore we seek to answer to various questions, for example:

- Should we negotiate or should we wait?
- Which and how many means should we use during our negotiations?
- When will negotiations take place, and how long will they last?
- What type of exchanges are we willing to give?
- What are our alternative scenarios, if we do not have the desired results?
- How is the other party planning to act, and how will we influence his or her behavior?
- What will the consequences of our behavior be, and how will the other party behave?

The realization of negotiation

This stage includes, for example, the answers to the following questions regarding our behavior towards the other party:

- How will we express our friendliness or dissatisfaction to the other party?
- How do we show that we respect them, or that we are ignoring them, or that we are rejecting them?
- How can we behave so as to persuade them to take our point of view?
- How can we impress or disappoint them?
- What style of language should be used?
- How can we create the desired climate for our relationships?
- How should we dress, and in which colors?
- In order to respect their preferences for personal space, how close should we stand? When meeting them, what should our distance be from them?
- What type of body language should we use?
- Which would be the appropriate social mannerisms during the meeting (e.g. eye contact, the lunch menu)?

From these questions, it is obvious that negotiations cover two different types of approach to problem: strategic and tactical. In addition, the tactical approach depends on the nature of the strategic approach chosen. This combination has been ignored by scholars and, thus, their proposed "recipes" can often lead to unanticipated results.

2.5 Stages of the conflict model

The model of conflicts that we will develop in what follows seeks to explain the way we plan our negotiation behavior. According to this model, the explanation of behaviors is based on the thought process of any person dealing with a conflict of interests and can be summarized in the following four stages:

- The formation of our initial desired conflict behavior.
- The determination of a power budget, which allocates our power reserves to our various conflict arenas.
- The examination of the efficient use of our planned powers, which are bound up with the existing conditions.
- The evaluation of the consequences of our planned actions and, therefore, the choosing of the most beneficial negotiation behavior.

We conclude that the stages of this model begin with the examination of the initial stages of conflict and lead up to the final stage of choosing a negotiation behavior.

Stage 1: formation of initial conflict behavior

This stage, which is analyzed in Chapter 3, examines the ways in which we behave once we have perceived a conflict. Some of these behaviors refer to the desire to act to resolve the conflict, or to the piling up conflicts, or even overlooking or forgetting them.

In case study 2.1, Alex will probably behave in different ways in each of the seven conflicts he faces. He will ignore some of these conflicts; some others he will wish to deal with immediately. For the remaining conflicts, he will consider his future behavior.

There are further reasons that lead to these behaviors, such as the perceived significance of the conflict and whether we consider we are able to handle it. By examining the way in which the initial conflict behavior is formed, we:

- Adjust our behavior to the facts of the conflict we face.
- Predict the other's behavior, which enables us to influence them from the first stage of the conflict event.

Stage 2: the power budget

This stage is reached once we decided to deal with some of our conflicts. However, our decision-making is incomplete; because we have decided to respond to a conflict without considering the range of other conflicts with which we must deal simultaneously.

In order to complete our decision-making, we need to know whether we possess the necessary powers to achieve our ends, and to estimate how much of our limited powers should be used in each of the conflicts we face. We should therefore develop a power budget (Chapter 4). This power budget initially depends on the significance of the field in which each conflict takes place. For example, we might feel insulted by someone's behavior. This insult causes a conflict proportionate in significance to the nature of the insult. According to the nature of the conflict, we will perceive an initial desire to respond (i.e. power use).

Let us assume that an identical insult comes from two different people: our supervisor, and a colleague. The field in which the conflict is taking place governs the significance and relevance of the conflict.

We reach this conclusion because we consider that an insult from our supervisor causes a greater conflict, due to the fact that he or she can affect our job. The conflict with our colleague exists at a comparatively lower level, since the field of colleagues is relatively less significant than that of supervisors. These newly-perceived relative levels of conflict that result from the estimation of the significance of fields influence the power reserves that we will wish to use in each of these fields of conflict. We would want to use our more efficient powers resolving the conflict with our supervisor than with our colleague.

However, let us examine a possible scenario. In the time during which the conflicts arose, we decided to move to another company: our departure from the situation is therefore imminent. In this case, the significance of the relationships within the fields of our current job and the relationships with our colleagues is equalized. We would therefore apply similar levels of power reserves to each of the conflicts.

From taking a 360-degree view of the situation, we can predict the way the other party involved will allocate their power reserves, which enables us to develop corresponding strategies.

Stage 3: conditions and efficient negotiations

By this stage, we will have determined the various power reserves that we wish to use for each conflict in which we are involved. These determinations would be enough for the immediate use of our powers, if we did not face the risk of being inefficient. Therefore, we need to examine the effects of the powers that we have planned to use, bearing in mind the circumstances. Efficiency is dealt with from two perspectives.

One perspective refers to the quantity of our planned power reserves, and whether they are sufficient, insufficient, or excessive. If they are sufficient, we are efficient; otherwise we are inefficient since, in the case of:

- Insufficient powers, we waste them without achieving our goals.
- Excessive powers, our goals are achieved through powers that are withheld from the rest of our conflicts, and we might be inefficient in these other conflicts as a consequence.

The other perspective of our efficiency concerns the quality of our powers in relation to the corresponding quality demanded by the conditions in each of the conflicts in which we are involved. If there is a problem of compatibility between the planned and required quality of our powers, then we should expect to be inefficient. For example, the circumstances of a specific negotiation demands special knowledge in a specific subject (technological conditions). If we do not have this type of knowledge and cannot cover that lack with money (economic conditions) or with the support of others (political conditions), then, if we participate in the conflict, we will be inefficient.

At the end of this stage, we know either whether we will be efficient in handling the conflict, or what to do to improve our efficiency. In addition, we have the opportunity to develop strategies to influence the other party's efficiency.

Stage 4: consequences and choice of negotiation behavior

This stage is reached when we are convinced we can use of our powers effectively in the conflicts in which we have chosen to participate. The questions we face at this stage are:

- How beneficial will our action be in each of our conflicts?
- What should be the limits of our involvement in each of our conflicts?
- Which type of negotiation is appropriate for facing each of our conflicts?

These questions can cause hesitation. Many may ask: Why would it not be to our benefit to participate in a conflict, since we have proven our efficiency?

The answer to these doubts is that the efficiency and the consequences of our involvement in a conflict are two different matters. Effectiveness examines the compatibility and efficiency of our powers; when we examine the consequences, we evaluate the entire range of pros and cons in the event in which we choose to act in a variety of ways.

For this purpose, we use certain criteria with which we define the losses we want to avoid and the benefits we want to obtain from our alternative negotiation behaviors. Through this evaluation of our behaviors, we can determine and choose the behavior that will offer the greatest benefit, relatively speaking.

In the event that some of the consequences are not satisfactory and need to be improved, we need to find corresponding strategies. These strategies make possible our interventions in elements of stages 1–3 of our model, and also to the behavior of the other party.

For example, imagine we can predict that our consequences will be unfavorable because of the other party's resistance. In order to improve our consequences before the beginning of our negotiations, we take care to decrease that resistance. Even so, we look to others to support our actions in order to dissipate some of our negative consequences (e.g. the decrease of the cost of the resistance).

2.6 Summary

The model that we will analyze differentiates itself from those currently in international literature, as it is apparent from its brief presentation.

In our opinion, we are not interested in dealing with one specific conflict; rather, we seek to deal with parallel conflicts simultaneously. The basis of this point is that, because of limitations in our power reserves, the achievement of our goals in a conflict is related to the achievement of goals in any remaining conflicts. If we use an extraordinary level of powers in one conflict and achieve the best results obtainable, it is possible that we may make avoidable losses in other conflicts. In this way, we introduce the meaning of balance regarding the distribution of our power reserves, which should lead to achieving the best possible benefits from the whole of our interactions, not only from a limited number of them.

This balance is based on our goals, and the other party's behavior. Thus, each one of us must form his own individual model of managing conflicts, and this book shows the way to achieve this.

Based on this approach, we are led not only to improve our benefits through passive adjustments to one existing model of conflict but, in addition, to active politics. These politics give us the opportunity to influence the structure of an existing model of conflict in order better to fulfill our interests.

CHAPTER 3

Forming initial behavior

Once a conflict is perceived, there are three initial behavior options:

- Depreciation.
- Action.
- Accumulation of the conflict.

The behavior that is chosen will be selected depending on:

- The combination stemming from the relationship structure – extended or limited.
- The cost of the conflict – high or low.
- The conflict ability – high or low.

In this context, we also deal with "incompatible behaviors"; these result in "lose" outcomes, especially for the party that induced them. Conflict depreciation is thoroughly examined to stress its significance, since it reinforces our conflict ability. This behavior leads to the avoidance of waste of our power reserves, enabling us to deal efficiently with our major conflicts.

When we perceive a conflict, we ask ourselves: Is this the way we have to choose, the way we should behave? In this chapter, we will define possible behaviors and look for the reasons that lead us to different choices. In this way, it will help us to:

- Adopt a behavior that is appropriate to each of our conflicts.
- Predict the other party's initial behavior, which facilitates our influencing strategy, even in the initial stage of a conflict.

3.1 Possible desired behaviors

Every day we perceive many conflicts, following which our behavior options are:

- Conflict depreciation – forgetting the conflict.

- Conflict action – dealing with it.
- Conflict accumulation – remembering the conflict in our future dealings.

Before seeking the reasons for these behaviors, we will first determine their nature.

Conflict depreciation

Whenever a conflict does not cause the desire to respond – not only at the time but also at any point in the future – then the conflict is *depreciated*. The reason for this depreciation is our perception that it would be excessive to engage in that specific conflict, or even remember it.

Conflict action

The need for *action* comes from our refusal to accept the deficit caused by the other party, and we feel a need to do something about it.

Example 3.1   Depreciated conflict

Over the last few days, one of our subordinates has been arriving late at work, which has created an additional burden on some of his colleagues. This subordinate faces considerable personal and family issues, and each of his colleagues in the department feels sympathetic towards him. However, those issues are expected to be settled soon.

In the circumstances, we turn a blind eye to his being late and our future behavior towards him (e.g. his evaluation) will remain unaffected.

Example 3.2   Conflict action

We knew that, during the next two days, there was going to be a considerable workload in the department. Every member of staff had to be there, as any absence would cause an additional burden on everyone else. During those days, two subordinates did not show up due to health reasons, thus making everyone else complain and comment that their absence had been planned in advance.

The following day, we asked for reliable proofs and decided that there would be consequences if their lack of professionalism were confirmed.

Example 3.3 Conflict accumulation

Tim failed to show at work on every day preceding a public holiday, allegedly on health reasons. Initially, we did not object to this, although we doubted him being ill; however, when the same situation occurred repeatedly, we asked for an explanation. (Otherwise we could have rejected a few hours' leave for the settlement of a personal issue, bearing in mind any previous absences.)

When John alluded to a health issue for the first time on a working day preceding a public holiday, this caused a general reaction in the department, as we were biased because of Tim's behavior. Furthermore, whilst the tension caused by Tim's behavior kept accumulating without proceeding to a response, we ended up ignoring the whole situation, as these episodes ceased without our intervention.

Conflict accumulation

The need to *accumulate conflicts* stands between the two previous behaviors. In other words, if we do not wish to respond to the conflict and yet do not wish to overlook it, then we note it together with other similar conflicts that have happened previously or that will arise in the future between the same or different parties.

Ultimately, the accumulation will lead either to our action or to conflict depreciation.

3.2 The three components of behavior

Generally, we are led to choose between conflict depreciation, conflict action or conflict accumulation by three parameters:

- *The structure of our relationships*: every relationship is structured in a way that includes conflicts and cooperations, together with a material or an emotional bias. So, we believe that their presence or absence within a relationship forms our behavior and, consequently, affects it differently when conflict arises.
- *The total cost of a conflict:* every conflict has a total cost, which is the sum of the cost of each conflict and cooperation present in the relationship.

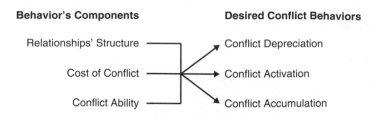

Figure 3.1   Behavior's components for desired conflict behaviors

- *Our conflict ability:* as soon as a conflict arises, we immediately build a perception as to whether we are able to deal with it or not. That perception might be the result of our existing "burdens", given that we are usually already involved in other conflicts at the time when we perceive a new one. Thus, the burden from the new conflict would be added to those already existing, which may make our engagement easier, or harder, or even lead us to avoid it completely.

These three components will be examined in the following sections. However, before proceeding with this analysis, it is advisable to present the method that will be used to interpret our conflict behavior based on those components.

The method, presented in Figure 3.1, shows that each desired behavior (e.g. depreciation, action and accumulation) will not be interpreted on the basis of just one component, namely:

- the way relationships are structured,
- or the cost of the conflict,
- or conflict ability.

but on the basis of a combination of all of these.

For this reason, in the following analysis we will first define each one of the components, and then we will discuss all of the possible combinations that would justify and relate to one of the three conflict behaviors.

3.3 The structure of relationships

The relationships between the parties may include many elements (extended relationships) or few (limited relationships). When a relationship is limited, the conflict itself is restricted to the unique event of a perceived deficit.

Case study 3.1   Catherine's work life burden

(a) Pressures

1. During the last two weeks, Catherine's supervisor has been assigning her additional responsibilities. These additional responsibilities mean that she has to stay at work until late, yet she is not receiving any extra payment.

(b) Ameliorating circumstances

2. Three months previously, for a period of two months, Catherine had to deal with personal issues. Her supervisor supported her by allowing her to leave work earlier.
3. Her salary is 20 percent higher than that of equally qualified colleagues working in other companies.
4. However, her salary also should relate to the fact that she has been assigned additional responsibilities.
5. Her additional responsibilities are part of an assistant manager's duties and have been shifted to her after the assistant manager left the company.
6. Therefore, Catherine has increased opportunities to obtain promotion to that position.
7. Should Catherine be promoted, her salary will be increased.
8. Following her possible promotion, she would often travel abroad to meet clients and company executives.
9. According to the information she received, those visits are tiresome.
10. However, these visits are highly compensated.

When a relationship is extended, the conflict is affected by all the elements comprising the relationship. Case study 3.1 shows the way our limited or extended relationships can influence our behavior.

Based on case study 3.1(a), Catherine's relationship with her supervisor is limited to a typical exchange: provide service – take money. What makes her perceive a conflict with her supervisor is the fact that this relationship is getting worse for her.

Case study 3.1(b) shows how Catherine's relationship with her supervisor is expanding with further elements.

The components in case study 3.1(b) unveil more elements in Catherine's relationship: it includes the past, the future, and also material and emotional deficits and benefits. According to this pattern, Catherine's relationship with her supervisor is *extended*; consequently, her behavior also is expected to be different from that within the framework of the *limited* relationship in case study 3.1(a).

However, regardless of the information in case study 3.1(b), which leads us to identify Catherine's relationship with her supervisor as being extended, it is very important to examine Catherine's perception of her relationship. In other words, Catherine could easily take only into account the evidence in case study 3.1(a), thus considering the relationship to her supervisor as limited. However, it is, in fact, extended, given the additional elements included in case study 3.1(b). The opposite can also apply: a relationship may be limited, but the other party may perceive it as extended.

Whenever we need to predict how the structure of a relationship will affect the other party's behavior, not only should we rely upon our judgment about the extent of the relationship, we should also consider the way the other party perceives it. This consideration prevents a flawed evaluation of the other party's reactions, since our expectations about whether the behavior would correspond to an extended or limited relationship might never be met.

The conflicts and cooperations mix

As mentioned in case study 3.1(b), Catherine's relationships include more controversial elements. This phenomenon happens quite often because, as a rule, our relationships comprise not only conflicts (deficits), but also cooperations (surpluses, benefits). Thus can be seen the need to acknowledge *cooperation* in the way as *conflict*.

> Cooperation arises when someone accepts the perceived additional benefit in their goals caused by the other side.

The information in case study 3.1 sheds light on the four kinds of components that comprise a relationship:

- Material conflicts.
- Material cooperations.
- Emotional conflicts.
- Emotional cooperations.

Material conflicts and cooperations

Material conflicts and cooperations concern objective, indisputable values and are not subject to personal interpretation (Example 3.4).

> ### Example 3.4   Material conflicts and cooperations
>
> A supplier intends to raise the price of products by US$200. However, since we are committed to not raising our prices, we cannot recover the increase in cost from our customers. The US$200 is fixed, and cannot be interpreted in any other way.

With this in mind, Catherine perceives a material conflict on point (1) due to the burden of extra work hours and the related drop in her hourly rate. However, her *material cooperation* is located on point (3), due to the fact that she earns 20 percent more than her colleagues.

Emotional conflicts and cooperations

On the other hand, there is information regarding strictly emotional features that cause emotional conflicts (e.g. belittlement, insults, dislike, mistrust, desire for revenge, and aggressiveness, not to mention previous or predictable shortfalls according to what has been reported in the previous section). Case study 3.1(b) locates the emotional conflicts on points (4) and (9) because:

- Catherine does not wish to receive any additional responsibilities (4).
- Traveling abroad would be tiresome (9).

Of course, many of us would disagree with Catherine and consider at least one of these points a benefit. However, she sticks to her opinion, thus confirming the subjective nature of emotional conflicts and cooperations (the same would not be so in the case of material conflicts and cooperations).

It could be asserted that *emotional cooperations* emerge when we are respected, accepted, liked, trusted and materially benefited, or we are due to receive benefits in the future. As a result, the types of emotional cooperation for Catherine, based on case study 3.1(b), are that:

- Her supervisor supported her in the past (component 2).
- She is chosen to execute some of the assistant manager's duties (component 5), which means that her capacity and worth is being acknowledged.
- There is a considerable likelihood that she will be promoted (component 6).

- She expects to receive a salary increase, in the event that she is promoted (component 7).
- In the event that she is promoted, she will receive additional increases to her salary as she will also have to travel abroad (components 8 and 10).

Discussion

The controversial data included in a relationship are recorded in Figure 3.2. On the left-hand side of the figure are reported the positive (+) features of a relationship, which are emotional (bottom) or material (top); the right-hand side of the figure presents the corresponding negative (–) features.

These controversial elements affect the way we behave, offering us negotiation strategies that are dependent on the formation of those data as they are now presented with the help of case study 3.1 (page 21).

Conflict control through a relationship's structure

If Catherine reacted to her increased professional responsibilities, and her supervisor avoided making a fuss about it, her supervisor would choose to limit and control the conflict.

Based on case study 3.1(b), the supervisor would try an easier path: he would increase the amount of emotional cooperations – due to his past support towards Catherine (point 2) – and also stress her future benefit (points 5, 6, 7, 8 and 10).

This strategy lies on the expansion of emotional cooperations (Figure 3.2); at the same time, it manages to minimize emotional conflicts on points 4

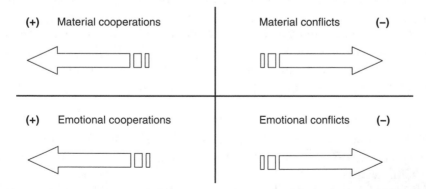

Figure 3.2 The controversial elements in a relationship

and 9, regardless of the shift of points that would take place anyway if the supervisor turned conflicts into cooperations. For example, point (4) may be the proof of trust placed in Catherine, and even a precondition for her upcoming promotion. To the contrary, on point (9) the supervisor may judge the information about the tiring trips abroad as unreliable, thus focusing on the fact that it is crucial for Catherine's career to meet with administrative executives of the head department. In that way, the supervisor adds one more element of emotional cooperation to his relationship with Catherine.

After this consideration, the supervisor might be able to assign Catherine additional burdens that she could not turn down. As a conclusion, if Catherine managed to predict the supervisor's actions, it would be better for her to avoid any negotiation in order to limit the burdens in her working life's (component 1).

Often, negotiations start within a climate of tension caused by emotional conflicts; in these cases, the strategy applied is exactly the opposite of that which we have just discussed. In other words, we tend to decrease the emotional conflicts and increase the number of emotional cooperations. Thanks to this maneuver, we tackle the data included in the lower right-hand side of Figure 3.2. So, if the emotional conflicts are high-level, then they play an important role in negotiations, allowing arguments to be handled with circumspection or even to be ignored by the more vulnerable party. It should be stressed that the process of decrease in emotional conflicts must be as swift as possible, in order to avoid spending too much negotiating time on past issues.

This strategy, however, can be avoided in two situations:

- When the depreciation of emotional conflicts "refreshes" the other party's memory about past episodes that they wished to be forgotten, or
- When the other party attempts to sell their past deficits over present or future benefits, which are usually excessive.

Bluffing by using emotional data

In case study 3.1(b), the supervisor could have purposely created expectations in Catherine regarding her promotion to assistant manager (points 6, 7, 8 and 11). This technique could be due to his objective to make Catherine take on the increased assignments during the present period (points 1 and 2). Then, once someone else is nominated as assistant manager, the supervisor could refer to the irrevocable decision of management in order to minimize

---

Example 3.5   Decreasing emotional conflicts

I am informed that a former customer of mine urgently needs products that I have supplied to him in the past, and which I have available in stock and ready to be delivered. The reason this customer had broken off our business relationship is that, in the past, he had suffered a deficit because of a faulty transaction. My former customer has alternative sources for the required products, but my offer would be the best concerning both the price and the delivery timetable. I know that, if I try to renew our relationship, my former customer will do his best to compensate for his previous deficit. In order to avert this, I avoid mentioning the past and focus exclusively on his ensured future benefit, thus expanding the top and bottom left part of Figure 3.2.

---

his meta-conflicts with Catherine – those conflicts arising out of other conflicts or previous conflicting outcomes.

Ways to expand relationships

We conclude that extended relationships offer more flexibility for handling conflicts than limited relationships. On the other hand, however, many of our relationships are limited, which creates risks for the outcomes and also can cause excessive demands and behaviors. Thus, when a party has a reason to avoid such developments, they are looking for opportunities to change the nature of a relationship from limited to extended.

In addition, the extending of the relationship is intended by one party when it aims to decrease the demands of the other party in present

---

Example 3.6   Expanding relationships

Someone buys a house from a construction company. His relationship with this company is obviously limited and, thus, he thinks that there are many risks of deviations from the construction company's plans. The buyer therefore tries to extend his relationship with the company, on the grounds that he may pass on his positive or negative experiences to a large number of potential buyers, who would be influenced and act accordingly.

> **Example 3.7   Emotional cooperation**
>
> A seller's objective is to sell a large quantity of products to a definite customer. For this reason, he promises significantly better quality and, in addition, expedient delivery of any subsequent order.

negotiations by promising future benefits. This behavior means that this party increases the bottom left-hand side of Figure 3.2 (p. 24), which corresponds to emotional cooperation.

3.4 The cost of conflicts

The *a priori* measurement of conflicts within social relationships is considered to be extremely difficult, as opposed to the *a posteriori* measurement, in which the cost of a conflict is directly connected to the degree of the means used, or to its consequences. This means that if, during an electoral campaign, there is a greater use of means than in a previous campaign, we can tell the difference by the conflict costs. We are also led to the same conclusion if we examine the losses in a war, or the number of participants in a strike, as well as its duration, the company's deficit, the social agitation, and so on. Nevertheless, these measurements are of mere historical value, since we apply only the *a priori* measurements to our objectives.

Conflict measurement procedure

For the purpose of measuring a conflict, we are going to begin from the conclusions of the previous sections. In these sections, we ascertained how the relationships between the parties are on both conflict and cooperation of a material and an emotional nature, and also that each element of conflict or cooperation is part of a larger conflict whole, thus influencing our behavior.

So, if we measure each intensity on solely the conflict and cooperation elements included in the relationship, we get a total value for each party with a minus or plus sign. A minus sign denotes that the relationship is conflicting for the party, despite its elements of cooperation; the plus sign signifies a cooperative relationship, despite its conflicting elements.

This process is shown in Figure 3.3, which includes two conflicting and three cooperating elements.

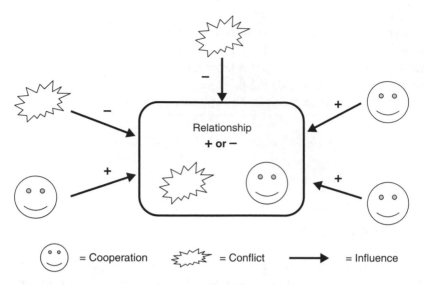

Figure 3.3   Measuring the conflict in a relationship

The offsetting of conflict and cooperation means there is a need for a homogeneous, reliable way of measuring these two controversial concepts, in order to avoid drawing incorrect conclusions.

Measuring conflict and cooperation intensities

For the purpose of fulfilling the presuppositions of a need for a homogeneous measurement of the intensity of conflicts and cooperations, we use the following two formulae:

Conflict intensity = Deficit cost × Deficit significance
and
Cooperation intensity = Benefit cost × Benefit significance

When measuring conflict intensity, the cost of the deficit refers to the difference between the desired benefit and the actual benefit (e.g. I want 100 but I receive 80, so my deficit is –20). Correspondingly, the cost of the benefit during the measurement of conflict intensity depends on the difference between what I could receive and what I actually receive (e.g. I could get 100 but instead I am offered 120, so my benefit is equal to +20).

Costs of deficits and benefits

Whenever the deficits and benefits are material, calculating them is simple; however, when the same parameters are emotional, their conversion to financial values is a difficult task. Case study 3.2 helps us determine them.

Based on case study 3.2(a), Helen perceives two material conflicts: on one hand, the low salary; on the other, the additional work hours, both perceived as financial deficits. So, the values of Helen's material deficits are:

1. US$300 because of her decreased salary – which means a –15 percent conflict, since she is paid US$2,000 instead of the desired US$2,300.
2. US$400 due to overtime – indicating a –20 percent conflict, since she receives US$2,000, while her overtime should yield at least US$2,400.

In case study 3.2(b), there are three emotional cooperations:

3. Quite an interesting job.
4. Expected acceleration of her promotion.
5. An expected raise in salary by 20 percent, due to her professional upgrade even if this were at another company.

Case study 3.2   Helen's conflict and cooperation

(a) Conflict

1. The company for which Helen works pays her a monthly salary of US$2,000, despite the fact that she believes her qualifications should yield at least US$2,300.
2. Most of the time, Helen works 10 hours per day, while the contract is for eight hours per day. Bearing this in mind, she thinks her salary should be increased by US$400.

(b) Cooperation

3. Helen's job is very interesting.
4. Due to the nature of her work, she acquires valuable work experience that could earn her a promotion in two years.
5. This promotion is expected to increase her paycheck by 20 percent. But even if it takes Helen longer than two years to earn her promotion, her experience affords her alternative opportunities in the labor market.

There is one question Helen should answer in order to express these benefits quantitatively: how much more money would she accept to work for another company:

- In a less interesting position? If the answer is US$200, then her degree of cooperation – how interesting she finds the job – with the current company is +10 percent (with regard to her US$2,000 salary).
- In which she could be promoted more than two years from now? If Helen's answer is US$150, then her degree of cooperation – in this case, the promotion expected two years from now – is +7.5 percent.
- That will that raise her salary by 20 percent more than two years later? If her answer is US$100, then her degree of cooperation expressed in terms of a 20 percent raise after two years is +5 percent.

From these calculations, we have managed to determine the first component of the formula relating to the intensity of conflicts and cooperations, formerly the cost of the deficit or benefit correspondingly within a relationship.

The significance of deficits and benefits

The second part of the process for estimating of the intensity of conflict and cooperation refers to the significance of each deficit and benefit. The question as to significance can be answered in two ways.

The easier way is for Helen to attribute 10 units to her deficits and benefits; the more she invests in each one of these values, the greater their significance to her. Accordingly, we developed Table 3.1, in which Helen records the significance of each of her deficits and benefits.

Table 3.1 Estimation of Helen's cost of conflict

Kinds of deficit or benefit (1)	Cost of deficit or benefit (US$) (2)	Preferences (3)	Intensities: (2) × (3) (4)
1. Lower salary	−300	2/10	−600
2. Overtime salary loss	−400	2,5/10	−1.000
3. Interesting job	+200	2/10	+400
4. Earlier promotion	+150	3/10	+450
5. Expected salary increase	+100	0,5/10	+50
Total cost of conflict: −$US700 or −35%			

In column (2), we have included the costs of deficits and benefits translated into financial units, as previously defined.

Column (3) clearly records how much significance Helen ascribes to each of her deficits and benefits by distributing 10 points to them, according to their relative significance. Finally, column (4) presents the product of each deficit or benefit cost, together with its corresponding significance. In all, Helen perceives a deficit equal to US$700 – a 35 percent negative deviation from her current benefits – which is the total sum of the conflicting and cooperative intensities.

In order for Helen to draw a conclusion on the significance of each deficit or benefit, she had to answer a series of questions, such as:

How important it is to receive a US$300 lower salary compared with:

- The US$400 deficit caused by the extra working hours?
- The benefit of having an interesting job?
- The benefit of the expected promotion being two years earlier?
- The benefit of the expected 20 percent salary increase as a result of the promotion taking place two years earlier than originally anticipated?

These queries are repeated for the degree of each deficit or benefit in Helen's relationship in comparison with all the rest.

Nevertheless, when negotiating it is crucial to know the other party's point of view in order to control their behavior. To determine Helen's priorities, we should either rely on what she says or simply predict those priorities. Prediction is, in fact, an advisable procedure for obtaining greater benefit or for checking the reliability of the other party's statements, in case they conceal their true intentions.

As stated, prediction also constitutes the more difficult way to assess significance, because it is based on scenarios about the situation the other party finds themselves in when the conflict arises. Each scenario can lead to different priorities and, thus, to diverse behaviors, as we can conclude from the following three scenarios for Helen.

Scenario 1: Helen has to tackle serious financial issues, since her husband has been unemployed for six months and her earnings have to cover all the family expenses. She considered getting a second job in order to increase her income, but this is not achievable: her supervisor keeps her at work more than eight hours each day. Based on this scenario, her current financial deficit is of greater significance compared with how interesting the job is or what may happen to her in two years' time.

Scenario 2: Helen faces no financial issues and is interested in improving her career, but within another company, one that will provide her with greater prestige and power in a leading company. However, staying at work over eight hours each day limits the time she has available in which to approach other companies for which she wishes to work. According to this scenario, the most significant criterion is her job description (i.e. how interesting her job is), which will help her to improve her skills. The next criterion is the overtime that limits her free time in which to pursue job opportunities with leading companies. All remaining considerations are of lesser significance for her.

Scenario 3: Helen has no financial issues and is very interested in her career in the company she works for, since she can cover both her professional and financial ambitions in her current job. However, she feels she has been treated unfairly when she compares her salary with those of employees with similar job descriptions working for other companies. In addition, the overtime she has to work causes difficulties in her family life. According to this scenario, what matters most is to be promoted at the earliest opportunity, thereby avoiding overtime; next come the rest of her issues.

To sum up, Helen's priorities would be different for each of these scenarios, which would result in different intensities of conflict and cooperation, thus producing three different total costs of conflict: one for each scenario. In fact, the total cost of the intensities of one scenario may have a plus sign and, thus, Helen might consider her relationship with the company to be cooperative.

Discussion

The measurement of conflict intensity is reminiscent of the measurement of momentum in physics: the product of the mass and component velocity of a body. The cost of the conflict affects our desire to use power in order to erase our perceived deficit. So:

> The higher the level of the perceived cost of conflict, the greater the amount of power we wish to use, and vice versa.

This method of conflict measurement offers the opportunity to limit or even erase the cost of a conflict without decreasing the conflict intensities, but by increasing the intensities of the cooperations. This leads us to the conclusion that:

We can patch up a conflict without really settling the conflict.

The settling of a conflict without dealing with the components of the conflict intensity but, rather, with the cooperation intensity multiplies our alternatives by the conflict handling.

This is quite important when we are obliged to experience relationship deficits because it is impossible or unprofitable to decrease the corresponding conflict intensities.

Let us take, for example, a train heading into a wall with a specific momentum: traditionally, to avoid collision we must stop its impetus by obliterating its weight (the deficit's volume) or its velocity (priority of deficit).

In other words, when the other party experiences a −20 percent conflict intensity, we proceed by partly or completely satisfying its demands to diminish or obliterate its conflict.

However, according to our approach, the collision can be avoided if we develop counterbalancing forces, which relate to cooperation intensities. That means that we increase the benefits (the counterbalancing forces included in the relationship) in such a way that the total conflict volume is satisfactorily contained, or even reduced to zero. The reduction of the total conflict intensity causes lesser consequences than expected, even if the conflict takes place.

In other words, a balance might stop favouring the conflict not only if we diminish the measure of deficits, but also if, instead, we create benefits. These maneuvers, though, do not lead to the desired results when the other party's deficits are below their bottom line; thus, the other party's behavior remains unaffected by the increase of cooperative tensions.

Example 3.8   Balancing deficits

An employee's monthly paycheck is US$2,000, which is below his bottom line of US$2,300. The employer improves the employee's working conditions in order to increase his cooperative intensities. In this way, the employer intends to avoid raising the employee's salary by US$300. Despite this improvement in cooperation intensity, the employee keeps looking for a job with another company, as his salary is always below his bottom line of US$2,300.

3.5 Conflict ability

We often go through the same conflict at different times but still feel the need to react differently. One plausible reason for this behavior is that we perceive our *conflict ability* in a variety of ways.

Power distribution balance

Before a conflict arises, we find ourselves in a *power distribution balance* concerning our existing relationships. When a new conflict comes about, it is essential to redistribute our powers in order to meet its demands. As a result, it is necessary to create a new balance of our powers in a way that does not worsen our position. Case 3.3 makes it easier to understand the topic.

The details in case study 3.3(a) lead to the conclusion that Harry must balance the distribution of his powers in order to cover his financial obligations to the contractor. Moreover, he has to move out by November at the expiration of his current contract, provided that the new apartment is ready for occupation.

Harry has many means with which to tackle this conflict, such as:

(a) Hiring an engineer to supervise the work and prevent any variation whatsoever.
(b) Personally taking control of how matters evolve.
(c) Suing the contractor for damages.

None of these means takes into account the way Harry already balances his powers. So, if he chooses solution (a), he will shoulder a serious financial burden. Solution (b), on the other hand, leads Harry to neglect the activities that will yield him US$20,000 within the next nine months. Finally, option (c) is risky because it could cause considerable delay in moving into the new apartment, which could create other issues between Harry and the owner of the apartment in which he currently lives.

If Harry aims at a new balance in the distribution of his powers to deal with his new conflict, he should avoid dead-ends as well as the erratic course of his deficits.

Handling low conflict ability

For Harry, avoiding these problems would mean adopting a behavior that is not his preferred option but is one that, considering his burdens, would lead

Case study 3.3   Power distribution

(a) Harry's power distribution balance

1. In February, Harry signed the purchase contract for an apartment that was still under construction.
2. For this purchase, he requested a 25-year home loan of US$120,000 and paid US$50,000 in advance.
3. In addition to this, he signed a US$20,000 cash receipt voucher to the building contractor that he is obligated to pay nine months from the date of the purchase contract, which means in November.
4. This time line coincides with the date that Harry will move into the new apartment.
5. The rental contract of his current apartment expires 10 months later, so Harry must have moved out by then.
6. In order to save the US$20,000, Harry and his wife must work hard for the next nine months.
7. If Harry fails to find the money in time, he risks losing the apartment and facing serious complications, since the bank has already withdrawn the money from his account and the contractor has already taken it.

(b) Harry's need to establish a new balance of powers

8. Three months after signing the contracts, Harry finds out that the contractor has not adhered to the initial specifications planned for the apartment.
9. When asked, the contractor falsely states this is not the case.
10. Despite the fact that these variations in construction are of minor importance, it is impossible to restore the building to its original specifications.
11. However, there is no doubt that these variations are going to affect Harry and his family's quality of life in the new apartment.
12. What's more, Harry feels hard done by because of the contractor's inappropriate behavior.

him to a power distribution that would achieve the best results. His behavior is closely dependent on his conflict ability. So, if he refuses to hire an engineer, personally take control or sue the contractor, he could find himself:

(a) *Ignoring* the new conflict, if he believes he does not have the appropriate power reserves to deal with it.

(b) *Causing meta-conflicts*: Harry waits for his powers to be released from the other relationships in order to mobilize them in the new conflict. For example, he sues the contractor for damages after moving into the new apartment, despite the fact that restoring the apartment to the original specifications would be completely impossible.

(c) *Settling the new conflict indirectly*: Harry involves people he trusts in order to change the contractor's mind instead of using his own powers.

(d) *Increasing his own power reserves*: For example, he could inform other apartment owners in the same building of this conflict in the hope that they will feel the same and be willing to contribute towards the cost of taking the contractor to task for his behavior. The precondition for this action is that the works in the apartment will be finished so that he can move out of his current home on time.

Undoubtedly, all these behaviors are far removed from what Harry would finally choose to do if he was not already preoccupied with other matters. So, it can be said that:

> The greater the burdens that we are shouldering in our existing relationships, the more our behavior deviates from the desired path when a new conflict arises.

The structure of conflict ability

There might be a material or emotional factor dominating the new conflict; thus, our behavior depends on how many issues we already have in the same field of action. Case study 3.3 shows that Harry's burdens are material, given that he has financial obligations to fulfill. If Harry takes on additional financial burdens, his conflict ability will be reduced to zero. However, if during the same period he becomes subject to emotional matters, without jeopardizing the fulfillment of his financial obligations, then his conflict ability will be better.

This is exactly the reason why the other party carefully picks the timing of the conflict, depending on how burdened we are with other issues. Thus, the other party may provoke additional burdens to reduce our conflict ability at the time when they will be in conflict with us.

The costs of burdens due to conflicts cause different behaviors in the parties of a conflict. Sometimes, we are able to predict these behaviors because of similar episodes that have taken place in the past, as presented in case study 3.4.

Case study 3.4   The aggravated general manager

1. One of the general managers of a big public corporation pays great attention to spelling mistakes and grammar when signing a document.
2. As soon as a subordinate presents a document to him, he focuses on finding any grammar mistakes.
3. Once the mistakes are identified, the general manager creates tension, explaining to his subordinates why he is right using rules of grammar.
4. Then, he corrects the mistakes in red and returns the document, only signing it once it has been fully and correctly edited.

This being so, his subordinates have a strategy when they want to make sure the general manager signs a document whose content could provoke a negative reaction. They ask him to sign a document when he is under pressure, purposely handing it over with several significant spelling or grammar mistakes. As usual, the general manager becomes angry because of the mistakes, corrects them and returns the document for editing. Finally, he signs the document when he has ascertained that the mistakes are corrected in the way he wishes *without really paying attention to the document's content.*

3.6 The desire to engage in conflicts

Once the analysis is completed, we are going to answer the following question: Which combinations of the various components (relationships structure, conflict degree and conflict ability) lead to which negotiating behaviors (conflict depreciation, action and accumulation)?

First, the analysis helps us to specify each of the above components according to their values.

More specifically:

- The *structure of relationships* can be *extended* or *limited*, depending on how many elements arising from material or emotional conflicts/cooperations are included.
- The cost of conflict may be *high* or *low*, corresponding to the total sum of the perceived conflicting or cooperation intensities perceived in a relationship.
- Conflict *ability* can also be *high* or *low*, depending on our ability to act adequately within a conflict.

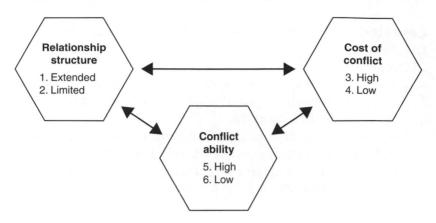

Figure 3.4   The relationships between behavior components

If we combine the specific components, we arrive at eight different combinations, as presented in Figure 3.4. Each combination leads to a precise negotiating behavior; the relationship of each combination with its corresponding negotiating behavior will be analyzed in the following sub-sections.

The desire for depreciation

Four of the eight combinations refer to conflict depreciation; their common feature is the fact that they include *low-level conflicts*, meaning point (4). As a result, the combinations causing conflict depreciation are:

Combination 1: 1–4–5: extended relationship, *low-level* conflict, high ability.
Combination 2: 1–4–6: extended relationship, *low-level* conflict, low ability.
Combination 3: 2–4–5: limited relationship, *low-level* conflict, high ability.
Combination 4: 2–4–6: limited relationship, *low-level* conflict, low ability.

Combination 1		
Extended relationship	Low-level conflict	High ability
1	4	5

Case study 3.5   Irene chooses depreciation to gain future benefits

1. One of Irene's colleagues asks her, as a favor, to train the son of a friend in her department for three weeks during the summer holidays.
2. After the first week, Irene finds out that the trainee is arrogant and creates trouble between the other colleagues.
3. Irene is about to ask a similar favor from the colleague in question for one of her relatives.

The low-level conflict together with the extended nature of the relationship means that we can expect to receive from the other party some benefits that it would be risky to jeopardize by reacting to a low-level conflict. In this particular situation, high conflict ability is not enough to achieve anything other than depreciation of the conflict. Case study 3.5 relates to the data of combination 1.

Irene waits two more weeks for the trainee to leave, assigning him duties he can carry out by himself without involving other employees. She obviously avoids talking about it with her colleague because:

- Her colleague is not responsible for the trainee's behavior.
- She does not want to put their relationship at risk, especially before asking him for the favor.

Combination 2		
Extended relationship	Low-level conflict	Low ability
1	4	6

In the case of combination 2, it is clear how the low conflict ability favors the choice of conflict depreciation. What would happen if we modified combination 2 to include Irene's low conflict ability by adding that her supervisor is *also* interested in the candidate in question? Her limited conflict ability towards her supervisor means that it would be difficult for her to refuse the candidate training and complain about the candidate's misbehavior.

Combination 3		
Limited relationship	Low-level conflict	High ability
2	4	5

Case study 3.6   Ted's depreciation choice

1. It is Saturday morning and Ted has finished all his errands earlier.
2. When he returns to his car, he finds out that another car is blocking his way out.
3. The unknown driver has left a note that he is coming back in five minutes and the flashing lights are on.
4. Ted suddenly recalls that he did the exact same thing some time ago when he could not find anywhere to park his car.
5. After two minutes Ted sees someone running towards him and apologizing. The unknown driver immediately moves the car and lets Ted make his way out.

Despite the limited relationship structure and the high conflict ability, the low-level conflict ceases whatever the reaction, as indicated in case study 3.6.

In this case study, Ted experiences a low-level conflict as the short delay of the unknown driver did cause an issue. His high level of conflict ability is based on the fact that he was free to behave as he desired but chose not to do so, despite his limited relationship with the unknown driver.

Combination 4		
Limited relationship	Low-level conflict	Low ability
2	4	6

In this combination, the choice for conflict depreciation is strengthened by the low conflict ability. In case study 3.6, if Ted met his supervisor while waiting for the other car's owner in the parking lot, his conflict ability would be low. The fact that his supervisor is present would limit his opportunity to behave differently to what is considered as civilized behavior.

The desire for action

The various combinations of components that make us want to take action are based on *high-level conflicts* and *high conflict abilities*, regardless of the limited or extended relationships. Hence, combinations 5 and 6 emerge.

Combination 5		
Extended relationship	High-level conflict	High ability
1	3	5

Case study 3.7   Holly and her new job

1. Immediately after her recruitment, Holly found out that two colleagues ignored the organization chart and interfered with her duties.
2. Should troubles arise in terms of these duties, the only one to be held responsible is Holly.
3. Regardless of that, Holly has to prove that she is valuable to the company; the interferences would certainly indicate the opposite.
4. In addition to this, she has been hired by the company in order to resolve certain issues in the fields in which her two colleagues interfere.

As we can see, relationship structure affects the kinds of reactions because, when the structure is extended, the use of powers is in accordance with the other party's expected benefits. This kind of combination is shown in case study 3.7.

Based on these details, Holly has *extended relationships* with both her colleagues and perceives a *high-level conflict* because of the risk of losing her job. Her *conflict ability* is *high*, because she can behave in accordance with the organization chart and face the problems that led the company to hire her, and in which her colleagues are interfering. Thus, her action is a given fact, but is also limited by the extended relationships with her two colleagues.

Combination 6		
Limited relationship	High-level conflict	High ability
2	3	5

The difference between combination 6 and combination 5 is that combination 6 sustains our intention to take action due to the limited structure of the relationships. For this reason, there are no inhibitions in terms of the means to be used.

We proceed by modifying case study 3.7; let us say, for example, that the interferences in Holly's duties are not caused by her two colleagues but an external company consultant. This consultant worked at the company before Holly was engaged. As soon as she was hired, he has been trying to impose his viewpoints in order to become indispensable to her in the exercise of her duties and to avoid interrupting his cooperation with the company. After this, Holly takes action without inhibition to stop his interference in her duties and with the aim of causing his removal.

The desire for accumulation

The combinations of relationships leading to a desire for accumulation share a common feature: the *conflict* is high-level whereas the *conflict ability* is low, which is ultimately crucial to conflict accumulation rather than conflict action. In other words, what is needed to shift from accumulation to action is the change of conflict ability from low to high.

Thus, when the conflict cost is low in the ensuing period, accumulation leads to depreciation and becomes one of the combinations we analyzed in sub-section 3.6.1, which include low-level conflicts. Based on these comments, combinations 7 and 8 lead to accumulation.

Combination 7		
Extended relationship	High-level conflict	Low ability
1	3	6

In case study 3.8, we can observe the relationships of combination 7.

The inflated bill is a problem because the company has set Phil a specific allowance for each working lunch. If he goes over the limit, he must cover the difference from his own pocket. However, Phil thinks there might be a

Case study 3.8   Phil is interested in the new client

Phil has planned a working lunch with an important potential client in a large provincial town. If they make a deal, there will be many opportunities to expand the range of sales, even within neighboring regions. The working lunch takes place in the most suitable restaurant for this purpose; there seems to be a good atmosphere, which makes Phil optimistic about accomplishing his goal.

1. Discussions about the detailed terms of the collaboration goes on until the waiter bursts into the conversation.
2. The waiter brings the bill and asks to be paid as the staff are about to change their shifts.
3. Phil gives his credit card without interrupting the verbal and visual communication with his client.
4. However, when Phil signs the receipt he finds out that the bill is US$50 higher than he expected.

mistake with the bill. Bearing in mind the high-level conflict and the low conflict ability, how is Phil going to react?

Phil cannot interrupt negotiations with the client to disagree with the bill; this could disorientate the client over negotiations, or even create a negative impression. For example, the client could think that Phil prefers to engage in "cheap" deals: rather than focusing on the potential deal, which is worth a great deal of money, he makes a fuss to the waiter over US$50.

As a result, Phil does not take action due to his low conflict ability; instead, he accumulates the high-level conflict. When the lunch is over, Phil returns to the restaurant asking for an explanation. His reaction is limited, since he perceives the relationship with the restaurant as *extended*. This perception lies in the fact that Phil himself might need the same restaurant for future working lunches with other potential clients, so creating large tensions would only exacerbate the problem in the future.

Furthermore, Phil's perception could be influenced by the fact that the restaurant's owner and the client are well-known to each other, which is ordinary in provincial towns where everybody knows everybody else. Accordingly, if Phil's action goes beyond the generally accepted limit, it could cause negative comments to spread very quickly in the town.

Ultimately, Phil might also avoid reacting at all and choose to depreciate his tensions if he achieves the potential client's signature to the collaboration deal as soon as they go back to his office after lunch. The kudos and the bonus that Phil will earn will reduce his conflict intensity concerning the extra US$50 to zero. Not only that: if he is in the least superstitious, he may also believe the restaurant and the inflated bill brought him luck!

Combination 8		
Limited relationship	High-level conflict	Low ability
2	3	6

The difference between combinations 7 and 8 is that in combination 8 the structure of the relationship is limited. This difference does not lead us to our desire for accumulation but, rather, brings about a change in the way we will behave in the event that we come to act.

Taking case study 3.8 as a starting point, if Phil believed his relationship with the restaurant's owner was limited (e.g. because there are other very good restaurants in town), he would have no inhibitions regarding his behavior.

He might also be led to depreciate the whole event for a variety of reasons (e.g. if, after the negotiations with the new client, he must leave the town as soon as possible, and if the company sent him back to the same town one month later, he would think it would be absolutely out of the question to discuss that specific bill with the restaurant.

Discussion

At this point, depreciation as an initial behavior is being completed, while the remaining two behaviors would also fit into the subsequent stages. For this reason, we are going to examine more specialized topics

However, first we will examine the ways for handling behaviors that are incompatible with combinations 1 to 8.

Incompatible behaviors: repercussions and handling

Sometimes a behavior evolves differently than has been predetermined by corresponding it to the combinations 1 to 8. In such cases, the behavior is *incompatible* and brings irreparable shortfalls to one or both parties. Case study 3.9 illustrates such an incompatible behavior.

As the speakers were ready to leave, the receptionist asked them to return the adapter in front of other company representatives. The speakers said the adapter had been left in the training room. This statement apparently did not convince the receptionist, who told them to wait until he checked the room for the adapter. They waited 10 minutes.

Case study 3.9   Two seminar speakers face an incompatible behavior

A large corporation is organizing an inter-corporate training seminar for its executives in a luxury hotel. The training seminar lasts for three days, and the hotel charge is over US$5,000. At the beginning of the training seminar, the speakers realize that their computer cabling system socket is incompatible with the supply provided at the hotel.

1. For this reason, they asked the hotel manager to provide them with a special adapter.
2. The adapter should not cost more than US$3.
3. When the seminar ended, the speakers went down to the hotel reception to check out.
4. Their taxi was already in front of the hotel waiting for them.

Based on these details, the receptionist's behavior was incompatible, considering his negotiating combination. More specifically:

- *His relationship was extended* (1): for the receptionist, the other party is not the speakers but, rather, the company organizing the seminar. In fact, the relationship with the company is a multi-relational engagement that goes beyond the training seminars, and has a past and a future.
- *His conflict was low-level* (4): even if the US$3 adapter had not been left in the training room, the value of its loss would have been zero compared with the hotel's benefits from their continued relationship.
- *His conflict ability was low* (6): there were many customers awaiting the receptionist's attention or standing in the lobby, and therefore in a position to notice the speakers' complaints and to perceive the conflict.

The combination of these points, 1–4–6, determines a behavior aimed at *conflict depreciation*, not action. However, why did the receptionist behave differently than would have been expected by this combination? A valid hypothesis is that the receptionist acted according to a 2–3–5 combination.

- *A limited relationships' structure* (2): perhaps the receptionist considered the two speakers to be the other party, whom he thought he would probably never meet again.
- *A high-level conflict* (3): because the adapter itself is of no great financial value, the receptionist's conflict cost must be sought within emotional data (e.g. he thought the two speakers behaved arrogantly or he disliked their native country).
- *High conflict ability* (5): during the 10 minutes the speakers waited while the problem was resolved, the other customers could have easily been assisted. The only matter the receptionist should have taken into consideration was to assist the customers: he should not have caused them the additional inconvenience caused by the speakers' complaints, which is unacceptable in a luxury hotel.

This combination, 2–3–5, leads to conflict action, which explains the receptionist's behavior.

At this point, it is clear that the receptionist's behavior shapes the negotiating behavior of the two speakers in exactly the same way:

- They considered their relationship with the hotel to be *limited* (2).
- Their conflict was *high-level* (3) because their honesty and integrity were questioned over a matter of US$3.

- Their conflict ability was *high* (5) as, during the 10-minute wait, they had the opportunity to adopt a desired negotiating behavior, without limitations.

Thus, the two speakers reacted; the noise alarmed the supervisor, who intervened and apologized to the speakers and all the company representatives. Despite clarification, the speakers prompted the company to choose another hotel for their next training seminar, and all this for an item worth US$3!

We often run into incompatible behaviors, causing dilemmas about whether they are worth facing or not, since they usually lead to shortfalls for all participants. In order to manage such behaviors, one must know special strategies like the ones presented in Figure 7.3 (page 167).

Conflict depreciation: purpose, strategies, limitations

Certain civilizations believe it is a failure or a sign of weakness for someone to depreciate their conflicts instead of proving how powerful they are, or how able they are to impose themselves over their rivals.

Nevertheless, according to our model, conflict depreciation is thought to be *the most significant of all behaviors, and the one that demands special skills and knowledge.* This point of view relies on our principles, according to which:

- Our powers are limited.
- We engage in many conflicts at the same time.

This means that the inability to depreciate tensions concentrates them into a parallel burden, and when that happens there are insufficient power reserves to be efficient in the most serious conflicts. In other words, it is necessary to "close" instead of to "open" conflict fronts that are of secondary significance to the total cost of benefits. It is true that the significance of depreciation, as a procedure, has been neglected or underestimated by negotiation researchers. They tend to isolate and tackle only one conflict at a time, suggesting techniques for a successful outcome – even within conflicts – that are, in fact, trivial. Our suggestion is, however, quite distinct: we firmly believe that accepting small deficits does not inhibit focusing on more important conflicts; as a result, we save powers and increase our conflict ability.

Apart from this, it is known that many low-level conflicts that are not depreciated at their initial stage turn into sizeable ones. Case study 3.9 clearly proves it.

Case study 3.10   Alexa's attempt to depreciate is misunderstood

Alexa is the supervisor of a research and development department. Last week, the work in the department slowed down while waiting objectives were being set for the next time period. As a result, some of her subordinates were underemployed.

1. Some of them moved to other departments in need of support.
2. Alexa did not react.
3. After three weeks, the department was restored to full activity.
4. Alexa had to face the bad reaction of those of her subordinates that had moved to other departments, together with the reaction of their corresponding supervisors when she asked them to come back.

Despite the advantages of conflict depreciation, such behavior could make us appear weak and encourage the other party to maximize their demands, as presented in case study 3.10.

At first, when her subordinates left to support other sections, Alexa did not react as their absence did not cause significant problems. In addition, she thought their decision reasonable. Thus, the combination of her details, 1–4–5 (extended relationship, low-level conflict, high conflict ability), led her to depreciation. Her zero reaction, though, was misunderstood by the other supervisors as a sign of weakness and submission, which they had the chance to suppress.

Similar behaviors are recurrently adopted in the case of "salami tactics", a method used to attempt to gain small benefits from the other party very gradually without unveiling the true objectives. First, the reason why these little steps inhibit our reaction, despite high conflict ability, is that we essentially consider the issue to be trivial. However, our total deficits gradually expand to a serious level. This is the problem Charlie had to deal with in case study 3.11.

Charlie not only does not react to Jacob's behavior, but also thanks him for taking on the additional burden just to fulfill Charlie's obligations. However, as time passes, Jacob's relationships with Charlie's clients start to adopt a more professional nature, and the clients begin to place their orders with Jacob. Despite the fact that, initially, the orders were accounted for in Charlie's sales targets, after a while Jacob began to incorporate them in his sales statistics. This turning point, which Charlie had underestimated, may lead to a downgrade and a reduction in bonus,

Case study 3.11　Is Jacob going to overshadow Charlie?

Charlie and Jacob have to travel abroad frequently to meet specific company clients.

1. Lately, Jacob has "accidentally" started to meet Charlie's clients as well, as well as his own.
2. According to Jacob, the meetings are aimed at improving the general public relations of the company.
3. Jacob's relationships and activities help Charlie keep his clients without his having to travel abroad so often; for family reasons, this was his goal anyway.

since the company achieves its sales targets at a lower cost, thanks to Jacob's activities.

Of course, Charlie could have prevented this turn of events if he had taken into consideration Jacob's combination of details, which was heading clearly towards action. Jacob's combination included high *conflict ability* and also *high-level conflict*, which corresponded to the significant benefits he could earn from Charlie's clients. So, regardless of the kind of relationship between Charlie and Jacob – extended or limited – Jacob was led to adopt an action behavior.

On the other hand, whenever it is in the other party's interest to create a depreciation or a long-term accumulation behavior leading to depreciation, it affects our negotiating data. In turn, this influence aims at bringing a data combination compatible with this kind of behavior.

Case study 3.12 illustrates this point, although the extended discussion about it occurs in the final stage of our pattern (see pages 166–9).

Since his first year of being the shops' manager, Paul has thought of setting up in business for himself. This idea springs from emotional and financial reasons: he would become more popular in the local community, and he would increase his income, despite being satisfied with his current salary. However, Paul is also somewhat concerned at the thought of running his own business. Harry has often told him that businessmen carry numerous responsibilities and that there are many risks. Although Paul has not changed his mind about starting his own business, he has not managed to save sufficient start-up capital during the past four years.

The lack of start-up capital comes as a result of two purchases he made. The first purchase was two years ago when, at Harry's suggestion, he bought a luxury car from a second-hand car saleroom, for which he paid

> **Case study 3.12   Eventually, will Paul become a businessman?**
>
> 1. For the last four years, Paul has been running a shop in a city of 100,000 inhabitants in which he was born and where he has always lived, with the exception of his college years.
> 2. Two important criteria governing his being taken on as manager were the fact that he was local and had acquaintances all over the city.
> 3. The mall's owner is Harry, who comes to the shop once or twice a fortnight.
> 4. Harry cannot call in at the shop more frequently because he owns two more shops in other cities that are up to 150 miles away.

a top price. The second purchase, which was more recent, was when, with Harry, he bought an inflatable boat. This second purchase was, indeed, a bargain. Harry was rarely going to use it, and he had only paid one third of the price, having taken a loan for the balance of the cost.

Obviously, Paul is not ready to become a businessman, and Harry is taking care to keep it that way. He manipulates Paul by exaggerating the issues businessmen have to deal with in order to diminish his desire to run his own business. In addition, he reduces Paul's conflict ability by preventing him from saving money in order to constrain his action. Harry's efforts lead to a positive result: the low perceived conflict ability is incompatible with action behavior in whichever data combination it might be placed.

3.7 Summary

In this chapter, we have defined the desired behaviors once conflict is perceived: *conflict depreciation, conflict action* and *conflict accumulation*. These terms would not be significant if they were not associated with specific components that affect the behaviors in question. The components were sought within the *structure of relationships*, the *cost of conflict* and *conflict ability*.

On the basis of the analysis of these components, eight combinations were noted, of which four lead to conflict depreciation, two lead to action and two to accumulation. A brief presentation of the individual combinations is given in Figure 3.5.

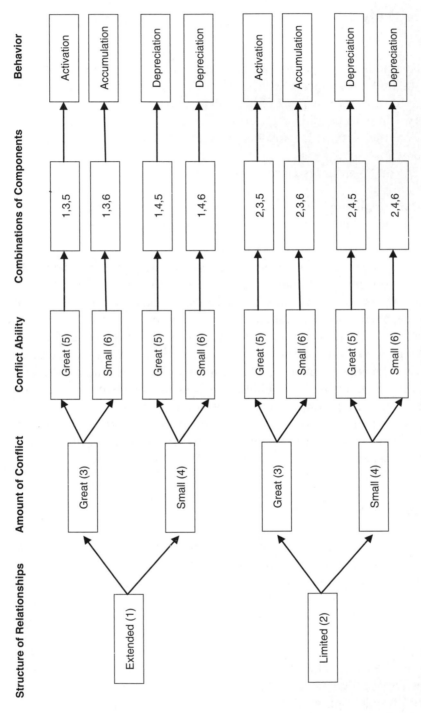

Figure 3.5 Combinations of components and conflicting behavior

Nevertheless, there are many incompatible behaviors diverging from these eight combinations and resulting in "loose" outcomes, at least for the party that caused these behaviors. According to the strategy developed in the following chapters, it is necessary to explain those behaviors in order to prevent them from occurring and to be in a position to handle them sufficiently well if they do.

Finally, we have paid particular attention to depreciation. The pattern of this initial behavior is covered in full in this chapter. Also, depreciation was judged to be very significant, as it reinforces our conflict ability and enables us to face conflicts of greater significance. In this context, we also examined the limits for this behavior, since depreciation could lead to unanticipated outcomes (i.e. growing a conflict instead of resolving it).

3.8 Moving on to the next stage

Our initial desire for action needs further thoughts before coming to its realization. A part of this information is presented in the next stage, in which the power budget is developed. In this stage we determine the definite powers which we will use in each of the conflict field we aim to participate. The process for our going to the next stage is shown in Figure 3.6.

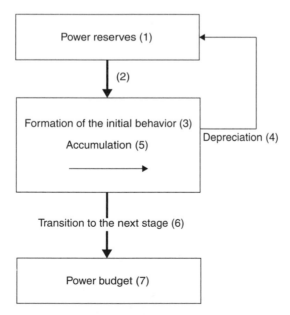

Figure 3.6 Path to the power budget

Figure 3.6 shows our available power reserves (1) with which to face our conflicts (2). The manifestation of a new conflict leads to one of the three reported behavior patterns (3). When a conflict is depreciated, no power reserves are used; the initial power reserves therefore remain unchanged (4). The opposite happens when action is taken; in this situation, we move to the stage of the power budget (7).

Regarding conflict accumulation (5) is concerned, there are two possible routes: conflict depreciation, or action. In the first case, we follow the path for the depreciation (4); in the second, we continue (6) to the next stage (7) to the examination of our power budget.

CHAPTER 4

The power budget

When reconsidering our behavior in a conflict situation, we take into account all the parallel conflicts we face in various arenas. This reconsideration allows us to safeguard and maximize our gains from the full range of our relationships, rather than from a single field. As such, this chapter focuses on:

- The different levels of significance between parallel conflict fields.
- The cost of conflict – which depends upon the significance of the particular conflict field
- Conflict ability – which refers to the availability of our power resources, considering their distribution to parallel conflicts.

In this way, we can build our power budget, which further promotes the development of an overall strategy. This strategy prescribes the extent of our intervention in each of our parallel conflicts. This chapter also discusses the flexibility of transferring power resources from one field to another, the symbolic participation in a field, as well as the concept of achieving synergies ($2 + 2 = 5$).

Once we decide to face a conflict, we need to estimate how many powers we are about to use, since, at the same time, we carry many other conflicts that also demand some of our power reserves.

If we want to be successful in our estimation, we need additional information that will help us to understand the behaviors in case studies 4.1 and 4.2.

Eventually, Elisabeth contacts the second client, and arranges to see the first following the meeting or else she assigns one of her subordinates to arrange the appointment.

Based on what has been written in Chapter 3, Elisabeth should contact the first client, who created a much higher-level conflict in comparison with the second.

Despite the fact that he has been picked for the program, Carl in 4.2 quits, hoping to apply again in the future.

Case study 4.1   Elisabeth finds herself in a reaction dilemma

1. Elisabeth is reading the complaints of two clients in connection with their recent orders.
2. The first client complains in a menacing way, whereas the second uses a softer, more contained tone.
3. Elisabeth only has time to contact one of them because she has arranged to participate in a management meeting.

Case study 4.2   Carl is changing his promotion plans

1. In order to be promoted, Carl has to take part in a special six-month training program (two-hour sessions three times a week, following his working shift).
2. Carl is extremely interested in his promotion and the number of applicants is high.
3. Carl has worked hard to meet the qualifications required to enter the training; he is finally admitted.

The controversial behaviors in these two situations are due to data that could not be foreseen in the preceding stage of research, since they refer to *the fields of relationships* and, thus, to the *power budget*.

More specifically, case study 4.1 classifies the first client as "small" and the second as "large". As a result, for the company – and Elisabeth too – the "large" client takes priority over the small one because of the much larger amount of profit yielded. The difference in the degree of significance of the corresponding relationship fields reverses Elisabeth's initial desire for action in the case of the first client, and so she finally contacts the second.

On the other hand, Carl leaves the training program because of unexpected family issues requiring his continuous presence. That means the field "family relationships" has concentrated a greater degree of significance than it normally would, thus absorbing a greater amount of power. These powers were withdrawn from the "training program" and "carrier" fields, which are less significant than the field of "family relationships". Once these powers are accounted for, Carl feels he is not capable of responding to the field "training program" and decides to quit.

In all, our desire to act and the amount of the powers we want to use depends not only on the data emerging from our initial behavior, but also on the additional data included in the fields of our relationships.

4.1 The components of relationship fields

The additional negotiating components to be examined within the fields of relationships are the relationships between the various fields, the conflict cost in each field and our conflict ability.

The relationships between the various fields: In case study 4.1, the "small clients" field is obviously poorly related to the rest, since any progress taking place within its action framework does not affect the progress in other fields. Conversely, the "large clients" field is strongly related to the others, because it influences both the company's profit and Elisabeth's benefits (her performance appraisal, her bonus, and so on). Accordingly, in case study 4.2 the relationship between the "training program" and "career" fields is significant, because the training program is a basic pre-condition for Carl's promotion.

The conflict cost in each field: There might be discordance between the degree of a conflict and the significance of the field in which it happens (e.g. a high-level conflict in a field of low significance, and vice versa). This means that the cost of the conflict, as estimated in Chapter 3, must adapt to the degree of significance of its corresponding field. This is also the reason why Elisabeth decided to speak to the large client rather than the less significant one, in spite of the fact that the less significant client caused a much higher level of conflict.

Our conflict ability: According to Chapter 3, whenever we engage in a conflict we automatically weigh our ability to deal with it. However, when this kind of ability is examined, taking into consideration the needs for power use in the rest of our conflicts, then our initial opinion might change. Thus, the conflict ability in that particular field relates to our effort to gather the amount of power needed for a specific conflict while taking into consideration our power budget in all the other conflicts. Now, if the power budget allows us also to tackle the new conflict, then our ability is high, and vice versa. On the other hand, when our conflict ability is low and it is necessary to face the new conflict, then, in order to gain adequate conflict ability for our new engagement, we have to withdraw the required powers from the rest of our conflict fields.

If Elisabeth had the ability to handle the conflict with the less significant client at the same time, she would have done so. Carl would do the same if he possessed enough power reserves to handle his family matters while following the training program.

Obviously, these components co-exist in every conflict, as the conflict itself takes place in a field that:

- Is or is not related to other fields.
- Is not equally significant to other conflict fields.
- Demands a different degree of conflict ability compared with other fields.

The combinations of these components lead to a variety of negotiating behaviors.

4.2 Negotiating behaviors within the fields

The possible negotiating behaviors within the fields are similar to those in Chapter 3, meaning they include depreciation, action and accumulation.

- *Depreciation*: Elisabeth depreciates her conflict with the less significant client and chooses to handle the conflict without further expanding her actions.
- *Action*: Elisabeth decides to take care of the large client by finding the required means for tackling the conflict, while Carl acts to face his family issues.
- *Accumulation*: Carl still hopes to be re-admitted to the training program in the near future, and is willing to use all his powers to achieve it.

To sum up, we are going to seek the components of combinations that can provide a plausible interpretation for choosing one of these three negotiating behaviors. The process is presented in Figure 4.1.

4.3 The relationships between fields

The reason we take part in multiple fields of relationships, rather than limiting ourselves to just one, is that we have the need to gain benefits of various kinds and from various fields.

The benefits in question are covered by *players* acting in different fields (e.g. clients, colleagues, friends, family members, suppliers, creditors, debtors, neighbors, local authorities, the company management, public opinion, and so on).

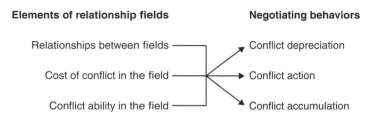

Figure 4.1   Components of fields and negotiating behaviors

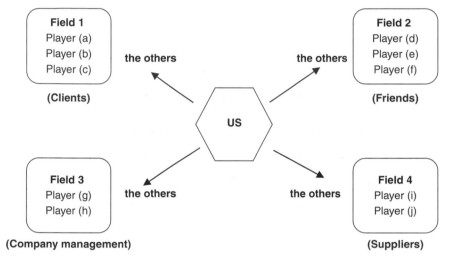

Figure 4.2   Relationships with players in other fields

Our participation in the fields can be *flexible* or *inflexible*, depending on whether an episode and our participation in it are the result of personal choices or they are mandatory.

Parallel relationships in various fields

Regardless of how flexible relationships are in terms of every single field, it is taken for granted that our relationships in more fields are parallel, as shown in Figure 4.2. According to this figure, we are placed in the middle of our relationships with, for example, four fields.

Each field is populated with players at whose benefits we aim. So, in field 1 (e.g. clients) and field 2 (e.g. friends), we are related to three players, whereas in field 3 (e.g. the company management) we are connected to two players (e.g. a supervisor as a subordinate) as in field 4 (e.g. suppliers).

As mentioned, the benefits emerging from the various fields can be quite dissimilar and, thus, the gain of these benefits may not dissuade us from claiming benefits from other fields. Nevertheless, the fields are often interconnected and, thus, deficits or benefits can be transferred from one field to another, which influences our behavior. case study 4.3 applies these principles.

The way matters turned out caused a series of shifts in multiple fields. The changes are due to the additional benefits X is expecting to obtain (e.g. expanding collaboration with Dan, or having more advantageous payment and delivery terms for his products, or setting quality standards for the products, and so forth).

Case study 4.3 Dan, his wife and supplier X

(a) Dan, his wife and their job-related problems

Dan and his wife have requested a home loan to buy a new apartment. The monthly loan payment represents 30 percent of their family income. Two years after the purchase, Dan's wife gets fired and unfortunately fails to find a new job for a long time. This event causes a financial dead-end and many family issues.

1. Dan has tried to find his wife employment in the same company for which he works.
2. Unfortunately, it was impossible: the company's internal regulation prohibits people in a conjugal relationship to be employed within the same company.
3. Thanks to his position as purchase manager, Dan has a very good relationship with the company's suppliers.
4. One of them, X, agrees to hire Dan's wife and pay her the same salary that she received in her former job.

(b) Dan rejects his chance of promotion

5. Dan's promotion in the company where he works is expected to be slow.
6. Another company in a different field is offering to hire Dan immediately.
7. The offer includes a 20 percent raise in salary and faster promotion prospects.
8. Despite these advantages, Dan is not yet ready to accept this offer.

Many of X's additional benefits may, however, run into conflict with the interests of the company Dan is working for, not to mention that some of them will certainly affect the relationship between the company and some of its other suppliers in the event that their orders suffered a serious decrease because of Dan's extra orders to X.

The relationship between Dan and supplier X comprises a combination of emotional and material data. So, on one hand, the emotional elements are based on the favor X did for Dan by hiring his wife, which alleviated his financial and family issues. It is important to stress that no one else offered to help Dan in this difficult period, not even the company for which he has been working for many years. On the other hand, the material elements rely on the fact that Dan's wife depends on supplier X for being economically independent. The relationships explored in case study 4.3(a) between the fields are represented in Figure 4.3.

According to Figure 4.3, Dan's wife is looking for a *new job* (field 1) and finds it in *supplier X*'s company (field 2). Her new job affects the way Dan behaves within *his own company* (field 3), and this behavior directly influences his *company's interests* (field 4) as much as they influence *the other company suppliers* (field 5).

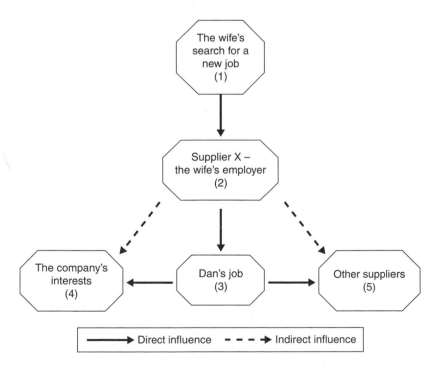

Figure 4.3 The fields of relationships in case study 4.3(a)

In other words, the relationships between fields 1, 2, 3, 4 and 5 are characterized by the "domino effect", which helps us understand the inter-action between fields. The remaining company suppliers (field 5) would only be able to interpret the sudden change in Dan's behavior if they knew how field 2 affects field 3. This means that they would fail to resume their previous relationship with Dan if their negotiating strategy did not include the relationships between the various fields.

This domino effect within the fields forms Dan's behavior in matters of the relationships between the fields, regardless of what had previously been discussed, as shown in case study 4.3(b).

Dan thinks that if X obtains no advantage from him, X will fire his wife. This would happen if Dan were to move to a working place in which he would have no opportunity to give advantages to X. According to this scenario, if Dan accepted the offer from the other company, then X would fire his wife and they would once more be placed in the same difficult domestic situation, as his increased salary from the new job would not cover his wife's lack of income. Dan concluded that he would only accept the new job proposal if his wife were to be hired by another company that had no relationship to his working position. Dan therefore asks for some extra time to think about the job proposal, hoping that in the meantime his wife will also find a job and they be released from dependence on X.

On the basis of these details, Dan's wife finding a job (field 1) represents the most important matter to the couple, becoming even more signifi-cant for another reason. If it becomes known that Dan's wife works for X and that this affects his behavior, he risks losing his job, exacerbating the problem.

If this scenario displays behaviors that can be considered "illogical", it is because the relationships between the various fields are not known. This is why, in view of similar behaviors, it is necessary to seek the additional elements completing the final picture of relationships between the other party's fields.

Significant and insignificant relationships between fields

It should be clear by now that the main division between the relationship emerging within fields is *significance* or *insignificance*. Relationships are significant when, during a conflict, the various fields build up strongly interactive relationships whose understanding depends on the details coming from those fields; conversely, they are insignificant when the fields are poorly interconnected.

The fact that the relationships between fields shift our desire for *depreciation* or *action* or *accumulation* of our conflicts leads us to ascertain the following:

> The more significant a relationship between two fields, the more our behavior is influenced in each field, and vice versa.

4.4 The cost of conflict within fields

In Chapter 3, we defined the total degree of conflicts by measuring and summing up the single intensities of emotional and material conflicts and cooperations. That value, in turn, affected our behavior as soon as we perceived the conflict.

Needless to say, the value might be right or wrong, in that the actual cost of conflict may or may not be different from that initially estimated. This doubt must be dispelled; otherwise, we might erroneously distribute our powers and finally adopt incompatible behaviors. Case study 4.4 presents this viewpoint.

Case study 4.4　Rose and her workload

(a) Rose fights to fulfill the order

1. Rose is a sales manager in a business corporation.
2. One of her larger clients, Y, promptly announces his intention to cancel an important order.
3. Rose has made her best efforts for this particular order; as a result, her sales statistics would achieve a bonus of US$15,000.
4. The bonus money would permit her to finance her daughter's postgraduate studies for the next two years.

(b) Rose shoulders additional burdens

5. While looking for a way to settle the problem, Rose hears that two of her subordinates are about to be transferred to a new company department.
6. Those subordinates are the best in her department.
7. If they are transferred, Rose's chances to win the annual sales bonus will be reduced to zero for the next two years.
8. In addition, the transfer of these subordinates will trigger more serious problems in her relationships with the rest of her subordinates.

In case study 4.4(a), Rose is related to three fields of relationships:

- Family relationships.
- Clients.
- The company management assigning her the annual sales bonus.

Rose believes Y's intention to cancel the order is because of her refusal to provide him the financial facilities he sought. The reason for her refusal was that the company is sparing with these facilities and Rose has used her allowance for other clients who had placed their orders before Y placed his.

It becomes clear that, following the transfer of Rose's two subordinates, the individual members of the team will have to shoulder a heavier workload, putting at risk the department's performance until the company replaces the two staff members.

If we take the notions of Chapter 3 on conflict measurement as a starting point, Rose's higher-level conflicts, sorted by degree, are these:

- With client Y – because he canceled the order.
- With the company management – planning the transfers of her two subordinates.
- With the rest of her subordinates – who will probably turn against her because of her inability to stop the transfers taking place.

What is crucial for Rose in order to handle the conflicts is to shift the above behaviors:

(a) To change Y's mind about the cancellation.
(b) To dissuade the management from transferring the two subordinates. and if she fails in that
(c) Should she fail to dissuade the management from transferring the two subordinates, to handle the reactions of the rest of her subordinates.

In the event that Rose decides to take the fields of relationships into serious consideration, then her action would expand as shown in the following analysis.

The significance of a field

How we perceive the significance of a field of relationships depends, to a great extent, on our subjectivity. There are people who tend to consider present rather than future benefits, and vice versa. There are others who simply accept running the risks instead of dismissing them. At this point, it is necessary to refer back to the section "Costs of deficits and benefits" (pages 31–2), in which Helen adjusts the priority of her conflicts by following three possible scenarios.

Similarly, in case study 4.4 Rose determines the nature and content of the fields with which she is connected.

(a) *Field 1, current relationships with clients*: The cancellation of Y's order will cause her to lose the US$15,000 sales bonus. That shortfall is worsened by the family needs in field 5.

(b) *Field 2, future relationships with clients*: For the next two years, the likelihood of her gaining the US$30,000 bonus (US$15,000+US$15,000) would be significantly reduced. This probable deficit becomes more significant when Rose also loses also this year's bonus, due to her family needs in field 5.

(c) *Field 3, the rest of her subordinates*: Some conflicts are expected to emerge as a result of the increased workload falling on the individual team members following the transfer of the two colleagues. Also requiring consideration is the probable financial deficit should the department lose the sales bonus. These conflicts will definitely exacerbate the risks in her future relationships with her clients and affect field 2.

(d) *Field 4, company management*: Management is in charge of deciding whether to provide or deny the financial facilities to client Y. The decision will affect fields 1 and 5. Also, there is the final decision relating to the transfer of the two colleagues, which influences fields 2 and 3.

(e) *Field 5, family relationships*: In this field, we encounter Rose's obligation to cover the US$15,000 expense, thus supporting the significance of field 1.

(f) *Field 6, the subordinates to be transferred*: The planned transfer will affect fields 2 and 3.

Once these clarifications are made, it becomes clear that Rose's most important – and possibly exclusive – source of conflicts is lodged in the relationships field (4): her relationship with the company management. Therefore, all her powers – as much those regarding Field 4 as those used for different purposes in other fields – need to be invested in changing the negotiating data in field 4.

In order to develop a successful negotiating strategy, Rose must first prioritize between:

1. Earning the current benefit of US$15,000 sales bonus, or
2. Aiming at the benefits due for the next two years.

Trying to satisfy both providing financial facilities to Y and changing the transfer plans for the two colleagues could prove to be extremely risky. However, Rose's solution depends on the cost of benefits she hopes to achieve by satisfying both of her two needs, as well as their degree of difficulty. That means how hard it is in Rose's estimation for the company to change the transfer plans compared with providing the financial facilities to Y. In addition to this, Rose must estimate the probability of achieving the sales bonus within the next two years even if the two colleagues remain in the department, and finding some other way to cover her US$15,000 deficit.

Hence, the negotiating strategy is built up by the feedback Rose provides to the various inquiries, although she avoids unveiling her priorities during the first stages of negotiation. By this, she confirms the more optimistic scenario of achieving both goals. Thus, her negotiating strategy lies in developing plausible scenarios on the basis of how things will evolve when negotiating with the management. Within this framework, she determines what is given in return, according to the course of negotiations, and prepares to use her powers.

The development of negotiating scenarios

Next, we are going to present seven scenarios based on the hypothesis that Rose gives priority to this year's sales bonus rather than to her future profit. So, before starting the negotiation with the management, Rose must ensure that Y is not proceeding with the cancellation of their order once he has the green light for the financial facilities. The list of scenarios is structured from the most to the least profitable.

Scenario 1: Rose points out that the relationship with client Y is in jeopardy unless the company makes an exception to help them. What is more, she negotiates putting off the transfer of her two subordinates to adopt more profitable alternative solutions. If the company rejects both suggestions, Rose is obliged to proceed with scenario 2.

Scenario 2: Rose asks for the approval financial facilities for Y, while giving up the right to facilitate one transaction with other clients within the following year, insisting on the cancellation of the staff transfers for those reasons. If management rejects both proposals, Rose will proceed with scenario 3.

Scenario 3: Rose asks for the approval of financial facilities for Y, giving up more rights to facilitate her transactions with other clients within the following year, insisting on the cancellation of the staff transfers for those reasons. If management rejects both proposals, Rose will continue to scenario 4.

Scenario 4: Rose asks for the approval of financial facilities for Y and accepts the exchange of one of her subordinates, who the company is planning to move, for a less experienced person. If management turns down both proposals, Rose will proceed with scenario 5.

Scenario 5: Rose exchanges the approval of financial facilities for Y for the transfer of both of her colleagues (their places will be filled with two less experienced people). The precondition for this exchange is the lowering of the individual and collective standards for achieving the sales bonus. If the company still refuses to accept, Rose will move towards scenario 6.

Scenario 6: Rose accepts her two colleagues being transferred in exchange for Y being granted financial facilities, with a basic precondition: lowering the individual and collective standards required to achieve the sales bonus. If the company's response is negative, Rose will move on to scenario 7.

Scenario 7: Management will not approve the provision of financial facilities to Y, and will not permit Rose to keep her two colleagues. Furthermore, they accept or refuse the proposal regarding the lowering of the individual and collective standards for achieving the sales bonus.

As we can see, the first six scenarios satisfy Rose's main objective of earning US$15,000. Scenario 7 is by far the worse, because it leads her to fail in achieving her current objective and contains serious risks regarding the failure of her future objection as well.

By the time Rose ascertains that the three first scenarios are unacceptable, by heading towards scenario 4, she will have ensured that more people become active in the field of conflicts. These people might be her two subordinates (field 6) or her remaining subordinates (field 3). The purpose of their activity is to leverage management in order to fulfill the best case scenario. Nevertheless, their successful activity presupposes adequate preparation for the maximization of their interventions.

So, there is a chance the company will change its mind about the transfers if it is suspected the transfers could diminish the effectiveness of both Rose's department and the department hosting the two colleagues. To sum up, Rose's opportunity to succeed depends on:

(a) Her ability to motivate her subordinates.
(b) The company's flexibility in seeking alternative solutions for the issue regarding transfers.

(c) The company's deficit caused by the ineffectiveness of both Rose's department following the transfers and the hosting department.

Should Rose eventually conclude that the company prefers the option of providing Y with financial facilities, she will stay with her transfer plans but rebuild her strategy accordingly. She will commit to mediation to decrease the reactions of her subordinates in exchange for having scenarios 4 or 5 or 6 accepted by the company.

However, if the management is sufficiently robust, Rose could apply greater pressure under certain circumstances before changing priorities. For example, she could lead Y to an immediate conflict with the company, making Y demand the same financial facilities offered to other clients. However, the outcome of this tactic could be overlooked because it only depends on how interested the company is in keeping that particular client.

If Rose ultimately finds herself obliged to reconfigure her priorities, she will most probably focus on safeguarding her future profit and give up the US$15,000. The final outcome will depend on the degree and resistance of conflicts regarding her subordinates and the company, which Rose has the power to settle.

Cost of conflict and field significance

The possible relationships between the significance of a field and the cost of conflict are presented in Table 4.1. More precisely, the table shows that field significance can be *high* or *low*; the same definitions are used to describe the cost of a conflict, although none of the conflicts arising between the preceding stage and the present stage is low-level. For this reason, this definition stands on the basis of conflict degree comparison.

There are four combinations of field significance the conflict degree, structured as follows.

Table 4.1   Conflict cost and field significance combinations

Field significance Cost of conflict	Low field significance (1)	High field significance (2)
Low conflict (1)	(1)–(1)	(1)–(2)
High conflict (2)	(2)–(1)	(2)–(2)

Combination (1)–(1): The conflict is low-level and the field's significance low and limited: the cost of conflict is even more restrained because of the low field significance.

Combination (1)–(2): Here, the conflict is low-level but the field has a high level of significance: the conflict increases due to the significance of the field.

Combination (2)–(1): The conflict is high-level and the field significance low: the conflict diminishes because of the field's low level of significance.

Combination (2)–(2): Now the conflict is high-level and the field of great significance: the conflict is at the highest possible level, since it keeps expanding because of the great significance of the field.

Analysis of the above combinations shows that the highest-level conflicts are formed in combinations (2)–(2) and (1)–(2), whereas the lower-level conflicts appear in combinations (2)–(1) and (1)–(1).

The final conclusion resulting from this is:

> The greater the degree of significance in a field of relationships,
> the greater the cost of conflict grows and the more powers
> we plan to use, and vice versa.

4.5 Conflict ability within fields

Our estimation on how capable we are of dealing with a conflict in a particular field becomes apparent once we have intelligently distributed the power for a specific purpose, without forgetting how much power we need to invest in all the other fronts. Often, conflict ability is not static but, rather, keeps changing proportionally to the shifting pace in the needs of power distribution within other conflicts.

Case study 4.5 reveals the difficulty in applying the rationalization of conflict ability within fields.

At first, Zoë felt honored by the proposal and considered it a good career move. However, after a while she began to feel more skeptical because a board member, compared with a simple member, has much greater responsibilities and additional duties. In her opinion, the president is in need of an additional trusted person around him as a back-up against the criticism of other members of the organization and the board. Of course, if Zoë acted as back-up for the president, then his adversaries would turn against her. She is more vulnerable to this type of attack, giving a clear message: do not do likewise unto others, avoid doing the same.

Case study 4.5   Zoë questions her conflict ability

1. Zoë has been a member of a professional organization for one year.
2. Her objective is to expand her relationships with other members in order to improve her negotiating capacity for professional purposes.
3. Until now, this activity did not present much of a burden, as it was limited to only one meeting every two months. Sometimes, she also took care of preparing suggestions for the meetings' agendas.
4. Last week, the president proposed that she should join the organization's board of directors.

What would happen, though, if these scenarios turned out to be true? One thing is certain: Zoë would need to invest many more powers than she had initially estimated so as to cope with the increased fields of conflicts. But does she have that many resources at her disposal? Could she eventually invest her power reserves in the new fields of relationships and preserve her conflict ability in each field (e.g. job, family obligations, and personal relationships)? Would the powers that were meant to be used in new fields of relationships lead her to conflict inability in different fields, ultimately causing her to collapse in those fields?

The answers to all these questions will form the basis for Zoë to start negotiations with the president. If she accepts the proposal, she needs to be equipped with sufficient conflict ability and be given professional rewards. If she rejects the proposal, she must avoid engaging in a conflict with the president; otherwise the motives for remaining with the organization would disappear.

Direct and indirect conflict ability

Conflict ability can either be *direct* – when we are able to tackle a conflict on our own, or *indirect* – when we need another field of relationships to support our conflict ability. The differences are presented in case study 4.6.

Case study 4.6(a) suggests that Theo should concentrate more power in the customers' field of relationships to deal with the production department issues (the domino effect). His conflict ability in the production department is non-existent, because it has not yet helped him find a way to improve the department's work and remove the burdens. He must therefore focus his efforts on supporting his conflict ability with other sources.

Case study 4.6 Theo's unacceptable workload

(a) Theo's ability is being overcharged

1. Theo is a sales manager who, during the last month, has had to put up with many customer complaints regarding delayed shipping and an increased percentage of faulty products. These issues cause significant trouble for the entire department in terms of handling the complaints and limiting the shortfalls. However, these circumstances are only temporary and will settle as soon as the new, inexperienced production manager becomes used to his duties. Until that happens, inconvenience will be part of the department's everyday life.

(b) Theo seeks new conflict ability sources

2. Theo believes that the sources that will improve his conflict ability are lodged in the back-up provided by the finance and public relations departments.
3. The financial management department needs to approve additional discounts and better payment terms for the customers in question, together with paying overtime to the staff. The public relations department must finance the required improvement in customer relationships.
4. The managers of the two departments refuse to fulfill Theo's requests, adducing budget incongruence.
5. After negotiating with the company's top management, Theo succeeds in raising the budget of the finance and public relations department, and his requests are finally met.

(c) Theo's additional burdens

6. In the meantime, Theo finds out that some of his subordinates are displaying inappropriate behaviors.
7. Only drastic measures can change those behaviors.
8. Despite the seriousness of the issue, Theo does not react as he would wish, thus making the other subordinates question his level of tolerance.

In case study 4.6(b), Theo builds his conflict ability indirectly after negotiating with the company's management, which approved his requests and intervened with the finance and public relations departments for their mutual support. This helps Theo settle both the conflicts with the customers through the other departments, and the departments through the management.

The only reason why Theo omits to react to his subordinates' lack of discipline is because he believes he is spread over too many fields. He therefore does not have the appropriate conflict ability for these additional fields. If he focused on his subordinates' lack of discipline, he would be removing powers from the other fields in which he is active. As he considers these fields to be inflexible, withdrawing powers is not an advisable option. Theo would seem to be trying to avoid the domino effect; if his conflict ability collapsed in one particular field, it would expand to all the other fields.

Degree of conflict ability

Conflict ability can be *high* or *low*, depending on whether the available power reserves are sufficient to face a conflict while involved in parallel engagements. This kind of ability fluctuates and affects the final behavior.

What is going to happen to Theo is presented in Case 4.6(c). When the production department ultimately resumes work to its previous standards and Theo gathers sufficient conflict ability, he will free up a considerable amount of power to channel into his confrontation with his undisciplined subordinates.

If, in turn, the subordinates considered the event, they would be surprised and incapable of interpreting Theo's reaction. At first, they would believe that their supervisor is showing tolerance or indifference; while thinking their practices have been accepted, they would suddenly find it difficult to explain his changed behavior. It can therefore be concluded that:

> The greater the perceived conflict ability within a field, the more we desire to take action in that field, and vice versa.

4.6 Behavior formation within fields

The preceding component specifications lead to the following definitions:

- The relationships between fields are *significant* or *insignificant*, depending on the degree of their interaction.
- A conflict is *high-level* or *low-level*, according to its initial cost and the degree of significance of the field in which it takes place.
- Conflict ability is considered to be *high* or *low*, depending on whether we believe we have sufficient power reserves to face a conflict once we

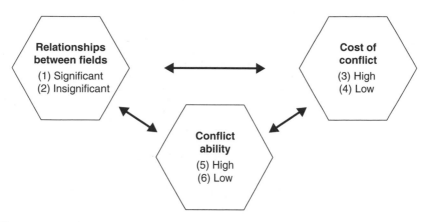

Figure 4.4 The possible combinations between fields

have weighed every single commitment in the other fields in which we are engaged.

Figure 4.4 shows every possible mix of these components, producing eight combinations. Therefore, the question we are going to answer next is:

> Which mix of components causes a behavior to lean towards depreciation, or action, or the accumulation of conflicts between fields?

Conflict depreciation

There are two combinations leading to conflict depreciation that share two common features: low-level conflict and low conflict ability. When these parameters coincide, we lose the impetus for both action and the accumulation of tension. The significance of the relationships between fields is not enough to make us change options, since the remaining two components – low-level conflict and low conflict ability – prevail when it comes to making a decision. As a result, the combinations producing depreciation are:

Combination 1		
Significant relationships	Low-level conflict	Low ability
1	4	6

and

Combination 2		
Insignificant relationships	Low-level conflict	Low ability
2	4	6

Let us see how combination 1 is applied in case study 4.7.

Based on these details, the conflict Eve is engaging in is low-level, because she is certain that the company will hire new staff to avoid facing huge shortfalls caused by the lack of personnel in her department. Of course, Eve is not the one to blame; neither does she carry the responsibility for the weakening of the department, given that she was clearly preoccupied about the retirement of two employees. Furthermore, she believes she has a *low conflict ability* that is insufficient to change the management's plans. As a result, she depreciates her conflicts despite the significant relationship between this particular field and others – more specifically, the ineffectiveness of her department and the relationships with her subordinates.

The relationships of combination 2 are fulfilled due to an adaptation of case study 4.7. Consider that the company decides to downsize in Eve's department and, since two employees are retiring, management will not

Case study 4.7   Eve depreciates her conflicts

Two weeks ago, two employees working in Eve's department retired. Until next month, a period when major company sales take place, these job vacancies will not cause much inconvenience to the department. However, Eve prompts the company to hire more staff; one week later the company satisfies her request.

1. After a while, the company's management decides to transfer the newly arrived staff to other departments that are in greater need.
2. At the same time, Eve is being promised that her department needs will be covered at the latest two weeks after the current hiring.
3. In addition to this, her subordinates have become somewhat nervous lately because most departments tend to cut down their personnel.
4. If the company does not keep their promise, Eve will have to face serious problems with her subordinates.

fire anyone. Eve's conflict ability here is low, because she has no reason to doubt the company's plans regarding the downsizing. Her conflict is also low-level, because there is no future intention to increase the work and firing staff. Ultimately, the other fields hardly affect her relationships at all, as any tension between subordinates is expected to be settled in one way or another, since the company will not dismiss anyone to suit its own purposes.

Conflict action

Action is mostly based on four combinations sharing the common feature of high *conflict ability* (point 5). The large number of combinations leading to action is the result of the large initial conflicts, coming from preceding stages, independent of field significance. When conflict ability is added to these details, we are led to take action in our conflict. The other two components of this combination – the relationships between fields and the cost of conflict – help to place the action sequence on a priority scale.

Once equipped with those priorities, one can choose the series of conflicts demanding action according to their power reserves and degree of conflict ability. Hence, there are four different priorities concerning action.

Priority 1 action

This lies on the following combination pattern and is presented in case study 4.8:

Combination 3		
Significant relationships	High-level conflict	High ability
1	3	5

The client's behavior causes Fred to experience many high-level and different conflict intensities. Fred's material conflicts are connected with the discount given to the client; the emotional conflicts come from the client's blackmailing behavior. However, this is not the most serious problem. It is not hard to imagine what will happen when the other clients find out that the tough negotiator is having "special treatment". And, if we push things a little further, we can clearly see the dire financial problems Fred will face in the event that he grants the same discount to the other clients.

Case study 4.8   Fred and his tough client

Fred owns a TV channel with an audience of three million people. There are four more channels covering the same area. Their greatest income derives from advertising, and the prices are fixed through informal agreements between the TV channel owners. However, one major client has begun negotiating reduced prices, gaining a 25 percent reduction on the price all the other clients pay.

1. Fred has often backed off from this client's demands, given there is sufficient free advertising space on the channel.
2. Fred knows that the client in question treats all channel owners in the same way in order to achieve his goals, and his strategy has been so far successful.
3. The client does not, in fact, need the money; however, he likes to be a very hard negotiator.

What Fred fears is a plausible threat. The tough negotiator is an employee of the advertising firm; he could unexpectedly move to another company and spread his negotiating tactics there. If that happens – and it is not at all improbable – his particular negotiating strategy will take the lead in the advertising field: in that particular area, information and rumors generally travel very fast.

Initially, Fred thought of adopting a common defense strategy together with all the other channel owners, but they have proved to be selfish, unreliable and unprofessional. Fortunately, Fred consulted his consultants and worked out a scenario capable of boosting his conflict ability to handle the problem. The scenario is based on the following steps:

(a) He refuses the large client's proposals, thus directing him to his competitors.
(b) He first spreads the tough client's techniques to the client market and ensures they all know how competitors submit to his demands.
(c) Ultimately, those clients confront the competitors because of the unequal treatment.
(d) Fred particularly exploits the emotional part of the intensities to obtain new clients.

Before applying the scenario, Fred examines the efficiency and consequences of his actions, which will be analyzed in Chapters 5 and 6.

Priority 2 action

The combination supporting second priority action is:

Combination 4		
Insignificant relationships	High-level conflict	High ability
2	3	5

The concept behind this combination is that it is inferior to combination 3 in terms of its poor significance between fields, as presented in Case study 4.9

On the one hand, Penelope's field of engagement is insignificant to anyone else (component 2); on the other hand, her conflict is large (component 3) and so is her conflict ability (component 5). Therefore, Penelope's intention to take legal action is predictable.

Priority 3 and 4 action

These combinations share two common features and one difference: a low-level conflict and high conflict ability, but not similarly related to the

Case study 4.9   Penelope fights against the public sector

Penelope represents a large radio communication multinational corporation in a European country; the capital of that country recently hosted an important international sports events. Within this framework, the public sector announced several Dutch auctions, with the lowest bidder being awarded wireless communication contracts. Penelope's bids have been turned down in many of these competitions, although she was in a more advantageous position compared with her competitors.

1. There is no plausible justification for the rejections that have caused her losses.
2. The deficit is becoming even greater: fast technological developments are causing the gradual downgrading of such products, and there is no hope for better days in that particular field.
3. Penelope's attorneys assured her that she has a fairly good chance of winning her lawsuits.
4. Her legal costs would not be very high.

various fields. The fields holding significant relationships take the lead over the field with an insignificant relationship.

Combination 5		
Significant relationship	Low-level conflict	High ability
1	4	5

and

Combination 6		
Insignificant relationship	Low-level conflict	High ability
2	4	5

To cover the data of these combinations, we refer to case study 4.10.

Based on this, the field of "supplies" is strongly related to others, such as "colleagues" or "company's owner" (component 1). The conflict is low-level,

---

Case study 4.10   Sean risks exposure

Sean works as the oil purchase manager for a shipping company. Three company suppliers sell oil at different prices, because they set different terms. Supplier 1 sells at US$97 per ton, giving a 40-day payment margin. Supplier 2 sells at US$98 per ton, giving a 60-day payment margin. Supplier 3 sells at US$95 per ton, for cash in advance of supply. Collaborating with the last supplier has caused a few divergences in quality and quantity, so, for reasons of flexibility, the shipping company usually works with all three suppliers.

1. The last supply is relatively limited, so Sean decides to call supplier 3.
2. During the delivery, the product proves to be of significantly poor quality.
3. Despite the fact that the company will not lose much after all, Sean fears the consequences.
4. It is possible that certain colleagues will expose him to the company's owner, accusing him of having made a deal with the supplier for personal gain.

because the limited quantity supplied leads to a limited loss (component 4). Overall, Sean believes his conflict ability is high, which allows him to push supplier 3 to make up for the poor quality of the product (component 5), by giving either a discount or a free delivery.

If we remove details (3) and (4) from Case 4.10, the relationship of the fields becomes insignificant, since Sean is not risking exposure. All the other details stay as they are: meaning a low-level conflict and high conflict ability. What is more, the insignificance of the fields does not prevent Sean from taking action, but runs it at a lower priority due to his low cost of conflict.

Conflict accumulation

The combinations leading to accumulation are:

Combination 7		
Significant relationship	High-level conflict	Low ability
1	3	6

and

Combination 8		
Insignificant relationship	High-level conflict	Low ability
2	3	6

The principle of taking the two combinations towards accumulation is based upon a high-level conflict– which prevents its depreciation, and a low conflict ability – which prevents action being taken. Hence, once conflict ability has been improved, the significance or insignificance of the relationship of the conflict field with other fields (components 1 and 2) affects our priority for action. Also, the highest priority is assigned to the combination that holds a significant relationship with other fields (component 1). Case study 4.11 covers combination 7.

For these reasons, Lea suggests any negotiations with the union leadership be held in abeyance until the union's internal affairs have been resolved. Once more, the details in this case study cover the combination 7 on the following points:

(a) The "performance appraisal" field has a *significant relationship* with the "staff salary" and "labor cost" field (component 1).

> **Case study 4.11   Lea must wait**
>
> Lea is the human resources manager of Z Company and has been directed by the management to change the staff performance appraisal system. The company intends to use this change to make salaries and productivity more interdependent, in order to reduce labor costs. Nevertheless, the change can only be successful if the union leaders cooperate.
>
> 1. At present, the union leadership faces internal issues that could lead to its collapse.
> 2. For this reason, the syndicate cannot negotiate over such a serious matter as change in the staff performance appraisal system.
> 3. Lea had insisted that she would experience union leadership refusal to cooperate in the change of the appraisal system because of internal union issues.
> 4. In Lea's estimation, these issues will be settled soon, even though no one knows exactly when.

(b) The cost of *conflict* is *high*, since the main goal is to reduce labor costs (component 3).
(c) *Conflict ability* is *low*, because the union problems deferred union cooperation (component 6).

If case study 4.11 is adequately modified, it can also cover combination 8, 2–3–6, whose differences are the insignificant relationships of fields.

More specifically, the company is targeting the reconstruction of an old-fashioned performance appraisal system that mishandles individual performances. The modification leads to an insignificant relationship of the "performance appraisal" field with the other fields (component 2).

4.7 Summary

At the end of this stage, we may finally know in which fields:

- We take action, and how much power we are going to use in each field.
- We will accumulate the conflicts until conditions become favorable.
- We are going to downgrade the conflicts, which automatically restores them to the preceding stage and to accumulation status.

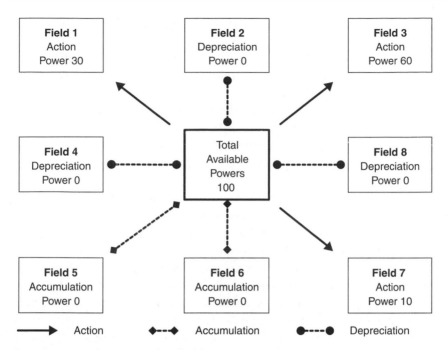

Figure 4.5 Behaviors within fields

Figure 4.5 describes the entirety of our intentions – (a), (b), (c). The central section records the available power reserves (e.g. 100 units), including: money, working hours, means of support, influences, rewards and anything to be used to change the other side's behavior. There are eight fields that are capable of absorbing the available power; therefore, in accordance with the preceding analysis, we are prompted to take action in fields 1, 3, and 7. In fields 5 and 6, we accumulate conflicts, whereas in fields 2, 4, and 8 we depreciate them. As a result, there is no need yet to invest power in these fields.

In other words, action in a field that has already accumulated conflicts presupposes an amount of power creating sufficient conflict ability. For example, how could it be possible to take action in field 5 by investing 20 units, when the action in which we are already engaged in fields 1, 3, and 7 absorbs all available power reserves? The only way to take action in field 5 is to seek additional power from a variety of means, such as in flexible fields.

Field flexibility

To take this principle a little further, in order to take action in field 5, which is under accumulation, additional powers have to be made available.

There are various approaches on how to obtain these additional powers. The most optimistic is to increase the total amount of the power figure (e.g. raise it from 100 to 120). The reason this approach has been called optimistic is because it is extremely difficult to expand power to that extent in such a short period of time.

On the other hand, the most realistic scenario is to withdraw power from another field of engagement or from a combination of many others; for example, subtract 10 units from field 3, 8 units from field 1 and 2 units from field 7. The withdrawal of these powers will lead to action in a field becoming partially or totally inefficient.

Partial inefficiency is the result of a moderate withdrawal of power; *total* inefficiency is presented in case study 4.12.

Obviously, any path requires the dedication of specific power reserves. Thus, Cristina has no flexibility in choosing a level of power use within her alternative actions to achieve an acceptable level of efficiency. For her, the situation is "black or white" without any intermediate efficiency levels.

Therefore, participation in inflexible fields means there is no flexibility for transferring powers to other fields. This enmeshes the powers in inflexible fields, thus maximizing the risk of collapse or domino-effect consequences in the event it is compulsory to reduce the power in an inflexible field. It is therefore advisable to avoid taking part in inflexible fields; rather, try to increase flexibility by using powers (e.g. through a *symbolic participation* in the field).

Case study 4.12   Cristina is enmeshed in inflexible fields

Cristina owns a small printing company. Many employees who have already left the firm filed an action against her for violating labor legislation, so many lawsuits are expected.

1. If Cristina fails to appear in court, she will be judged *in absentia* with dreadful consequences.
2. The same thing will happen if she appears in court without the required amount of powers.
3. Cristina's powers consist of money, time, legal support and cooperation with third parties.
4. Alternatively, Cristina can reach a compromise with the employees. However, this action also demands distribution of powers.

Symbolic participation in a field

There are many times that we do not possess sufficient powers or we simply do not intend to participate more actively in a field. Nevertheless, being absent from a field might cause deficits or hamper our future engagement in it. These are situations in which we choose a *symbolic* type of action, as explained in case study 4.13, which is based on Case Study 4.5 (page 68).

Since Chris does not yet feel ready to make "the big leap", he chooses a symbolic participation in this field. For the time being, he prefers to achieve his present goals, such as extending public relations, being informed about job opportunities, improving his CV as a member of the organization. and so on. Moreover, the present symbolic participation will play an important role in the future, when he will feel ready to invest more resources.

Achieving synergies in fields: 2 + 2 = 5

When dealing with a conflict, it is often possible to achieve proportionally greater results than the means available. This is the case, for example, when someone with 100 power units succeeds in obtaining 200 power units when the expected benefit was 130.

The interpretation of similar cases is based on the fulfillment of a *positive synergy* (i.e. the sum of the component resources produces larger benefits than those expected). All positive synergies are expressed by the equation: $2 + 2 = 5$ and can be fulfilled in a variety of ways. Let us focus on case study 4.14.

Case study 4.13   Chris chooses his symbolic action

Chris is the member of an important professional organization and a subscriber to its journal. His participation presupposes a non-expensive annual fee and annual meetings or unscheduled events devised by members. The journal informs any subscriber about professional opportunities and developments, while the meetings present good opportunities to extend public relations.

1. The journal's editor asks Chris to write an article to promote his ideas.
2. However, Chris does not feel ready to take this step.

Case study 4.14   Adam wants to be hired at X Company

Despite the fact that Adam is fully qualified and the interview went well, the company still has reservations about the final decision. The main reason for their reservations is that there are five more candidates for this position.

1. As soon as Adam hears this, he asks Y to back him up.
2. Y has a friendly relationship with Adam, but is also an important customer of X and knows the managers.
3. X's general manager accepts Y's intervention and hires Adam, with the expectation of obtaining future benefits from Y.

This case study shows how one player in Y's "friendly relationship" field was used in the "professional relationship" field in such a way that a positive synergy emerged.

Synergies can also acquire a minus sign, giving the equation: $2 + 2 = 3$. Let us change the information in point 3 of case study 4.14. Adam is not hired because of Y's involvement. Once Y's interest in Adam's situation became obvious, the general manager feared that Adam could leak confidential information about the company's customer price lists.

So, although Adam was seemingly supported by Y, he ultimately achieved worse results than would have been the case had he not received any help.

Towards the next stage

At the end of this stage, our decision on whether to depreciate, accumulate or take action in conflicts is definitive. In addition, the powers to be used in each conflict will have been determined. Action will be taken in the case of accumulated conflicts when conflict ability is sufficiently strong to allow steps to be taken. So, the power budget is set and will be adhered to so as to avoid domino-effect consequences.

Figure 4.6 continues and completes Figure 3.6. According to Figure 4.6, the desire for conflict action is recorded at point (8), since the intention to use power is reduced to zero and returns to the preceding stage of *formation of the initial conflict behavior* (point 3). How the conflicts will evolve from this point on depends on the dominant details of the preceding stage,

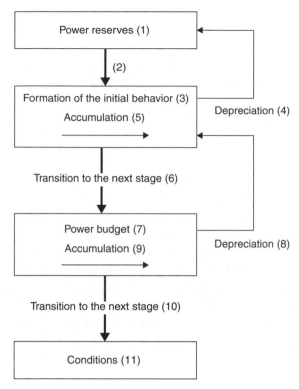

Figure 4.6 The transition to the stage of conditions

so they can be fully depreciated (point 4), or accumulated (point 5), or return to the agenda for action to be taken (point 6).

The accumulation of conflicts is depicted on point (9), while their probable action process lies in the development of our conflict ability. Finally, the transition to the conditions stage (point 11) appears in point (10). The consideration of conditions is essential, since our intention for action in a conflict field, with the determined powers, does not necessarily assure our efficiency.

CHAPTER 5

Conditions and efficiency

Our efficiency depends on whether our power reserves are sufficient and compatible, and on the potential reactions of the other parties. All of these are affected by financial, political, time, cultural, legal, technical, and complementary conditions. The identification of these conditions could confirm the efficiency of our plans, if there were only one predominant type of condition in each conflict. However, since this is not usually the case, we need to define the "mix of conditions." In every possible mix there is one type of condition that prevails, while the other types co-exist with varying degrees of influence in that particular conflict. In order to improve our negotiating strategy, we need to adjust or influence the given mix of conditions. In this way, we enable the achievement of synergies (2 + 2 = 5), as well as the assessment and influence of the other party's efficiency.

5.1 The sources of efficiency

So far, we have defined the conflicts we are interested in tackling and the power serving this purpose. Determining the possible parameters, though, does not ensure our efficiency; this is the subject of this chapter. Our negotiation efficiency depends on three facts:

- Having sufficient of the powers we plan to use in the conflict field.
- The qualitative compatibility of our planned powers, which is required by each particular conflict field.
- The other party's behavior, which could modify the previous two points – namely, the powers' quantitative and/or qualitative requirements for achieving efficiency in the conflict field.

These three points must be well-determined before the realization of our intentions, in order to avoid using power in vain or heading towards inefficiency.

Case study 5.1   Peter is discredited

Peter, the owner of a medium-sized business, is discredited by a competitor. This information comes to him from three of his own clients. Peter is willing to take action with regard to what has already inflicted a US$70,000 loss to his business, and also damage to his reputation and feelings.

1. Peter is confident about facing the conflict through legal action, meaning that he intends to file a lawsuit.
2. For this purpose, he can afford US$30,000.
3. The legal action is expected to last four years.
4. To win the litigation, Peter needs reliable witnesses who will confirm that he was discredited, together with an equally reliable, trustworthy lawyer.

Power quantity and efficiency

Case study 5.1 simplifies the analysis of connections between power quantity and efficiency.

In other words, Peter's efficiency depends on whether he has available a *sufficient* amount of power to invest in the entire process, meaning:

(a) US$30,000.
(b) The appropriate number of defense witnesses.
(c) The ability to support his witnesses for four years.
(d) The ability to afford a reliable, trustworthy lawyer.

However, if the conflict required more power than Peter was able to give – (a), (b), (c) and (d) – he would certainly be inefficient (i.e. if the conflict required US$50,000, or if he needed to present 10 witnesses instead of the three he has available). In this case, the risk of failure would be due to *insufficient* power reserves.

But, what if Peter wished to engage in that conflict anyway? Then, in order to be successful, he should withdraw the missing power reserves from other fields of relationships, with the possible following consequences:

(a) *No consequence at all*: if Peter subtracted surplus power from other fields to invest it in the present conflict with his competitor.

(b) *Reduced efficiency*: if the power was withdrawn from flexible fields, as Peter would eventually return the power to those fields when the conflict came to an end.

(c) *Total inefficiency or even suspension of action*: if Peter withdraw power from inflexible fields, because he would most probably not be able to achieve his objectives at all, or would be forced to cease any activity in those fields whatsoever.

In addition to these scenarios, inefficiency is also the result of the waste of power, meaning *excessive* use of power. Such a waste deprives other conflicts, thus jeopardizing efficiency or even the initial engagement in those conflicts. Let us examine the situations in which Peter could face this problem:

(a) In order to ensure the greatest possible number of supporters for his litigation, Peter decides to grant excessive concessions to the clients that support him (i.e. huge discounts, payment facilities, priority of orders, and so on). The concessions cause him financial problems that, by the time the four-year legal action is finished, will amount to US$10,000.

(b) Similar concessions displease other clients who cannot or do not wish to take part in his litigation. The dissatisfaction may arise because they are being treated unequally, or due to the fact that Peter's favored clients are competitors who have acquired competitive advantages. So, those who do not put up with his unequal treatment reduce or cease their transactions with Peter, thus increasing his financial deficit, estimated at US$30,000 for the next four years (until the end of the conflict).

What is worth underlining at this point is that inefficiency also occurs when strategies that require more power reserves are erroneously used instead of strategies that would lead to the same result by using less power reserves.

For example, Peter might have succeeded by having his competitor indemnify him in such a way as to cover all his financial and emotional shortfalls, but he still insisted on proceeding with the litigation and facing the possible consequences.

Figure 5.1 deals with these concepts, providing a schematic analysis of efficiency concerning the quantity of powers. According to Figure 5.1, the available power (1) can be: sufficient (2); efficient (3); excessive (4); or insufficient (5).

In case of excessive power (4), the surplus is withdrawn (6) so as to achieve power sufficiency (2). The withdrawn powers, in their turn, form

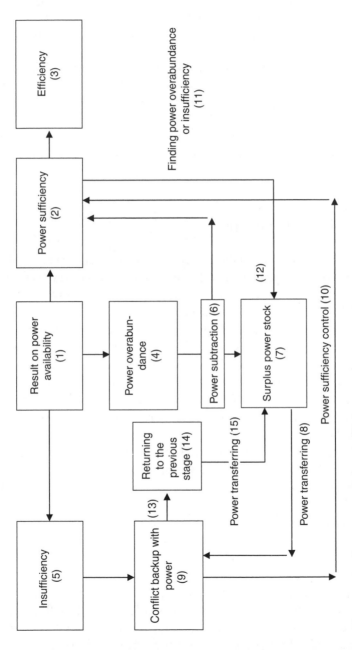

Figure 5.1 Power quantity and efficiency

a surplus power stock (7) channeled into any conflict in need of extra power (9) to make up for their inefficiency (5). Once strengthened, the conflicts are scanned for power sufficiency (10), and, if found, (2) it brings efficiency (3). Conversely, in case of insufficiency (11), we return to the preceding point (9).

If that point cannot gather sufficient powers, the conflict (13) shifts back to the preceding stage of the model (14), which means the power budget is in a state of accumulation. So, the power meant to be invested in that particular conflict is transferred (15) to the surplus power stock (7) and applied with maximum effect. Of course, when this checking process (11) gives excessive power, the surplus power (12) is added to the corresponding stock (7).

Power quality and efficiency

Mostly, participating efficiently in a conflict presupposes the use of different kinds of powers, not just one. In other words, there is no way that a conflict may require only money, or knowledge or third-party support to be dealt with; instead, it requires a mixture of all. Consequently, efficiency presupposes the availability of a variety of kinds of powers compatible with each of the conflict's demands. This was precisely Peter's case in case study 5.1, where he needed not just one kind of power, but a mix of more (i.e. money, proofs, supporting time and legal knowledge) in order to cope with the confrontation. Therefore, if Peter only had in stock "discredit" proofs and supporting time, the absence of any other element means that he would have failed.

However, the indispensable mixture is not always predetermined, which makes efficiency dependent on the ability to adapt to the new power requirements of each particular mix. Case study 5.2 refers to this specific situation.

The reason why Carl turned down the offer is because he did not need the money; besides, he preferred the fixed monthly income of the rent to a US$210,000 investment in the absence of current interesting investment offerings. Moreover, he firmly believed the real estate value would increase over the next year, which would allow an increase in the rent as well.

Jessica asks people if they know why Carl is urgently selling his apartment, and proceeds with a negotiation that will ultimately lower the actual commercial value by 5 percent and set the price at US$190,000.

It is clear, then, that the goals, the negotiating behaviors, and the final outcome have been severely influenced by *objective data*. These data were

---

Case study 5.2   Jessica and the purchase of Carl's apartment

(a) Jessica wants to buy Carl's property

Jessica rents an apartment that is owned by Carl. In early March, Jessica proposes to Carl that she buy the apartment from him. Her idea is completely unexpected, as Carl had displayed no interest in selling the apartment.

1. However, Jessica's final offer stops at US$210,000.
2. This price exceeds the actual commercial value of the apartment by 5 percent.
3. There are personal reasons why Jessica is really keen to buy the apartment.
4. Carl rejects Jessica's final offer on the basis that he has no intention of selling his property whatsoever.

(b) Carl wants to sell his property to Jessica

5. Four months later, a member of Carl's family is struck down by a grave illness and Carl, who must pay for the treatment, finds himself in the middle of a serious financial problem.
6. Carl decides to sell the apartment, which Jessica rents from him, immediately because he is in desperate need of money.
7. The average selling period to the actual commercial value is up to three months (time needed to find a purchaser).
8. So, he calls Jessica and lets her know he accepts her last offer.

---

independent of the action and desires of the parties, who adapted to them structuring their own power mix sufficiently well to obtain them the best possible results.

Efficiency and the behavior of the other parties

In case studies 5.1 and 5.2, what would have happened to the power quantity and power mix Peter, Jessica and Carl had available if they had had no adversaries? However, in conflict situations and in negotiations there are usually at least two parties. The quantity and mix of power would have been different. Nevertheless, the presence and co-estimation of an adversary while dealing with a conflict is unavoidable, since it enriches the negotiating process with new data.

On the basis of case study 5.1, Peter ought to take his competitor's reaction into consideration before the very start of the conflict, as it could change the power quantity or mix required to achieve efficiency. For example, the competitor could choose to seek his own supporters against Peter's accusation, or merely ensure the presence of a strong legal team.

Accordingly, in case study 5.2, the way Jessica and Carl behave affects the outcome of the two different negotiations:

- In case study 5.2(a), Jessica failed to buy the apartment because of Carl's behavior, even when she offered more than the property's actual value.
- In case study 5.2(b), Carl had to sell the apartment at a lower commercial price because of Jessica's negotiating behavior.

Figure 5.2 presents the process undergone by parties A and B, who adapt their behavior in accordance with the other party's data after having thoroughly examined not only their own situation (1 and 2), but also that of the other party as well (3 and 4).

The facts emerging from the analysis of Figure 5.2 are evident in Jessica's choice to negotiate over the price of the apartment based on Carl's data (his urgent need to sell the property), and to overlook the market value of the real estate. If Jessica had not heard about Carl's family situation, she would have agreed to buy at a different final selling price.

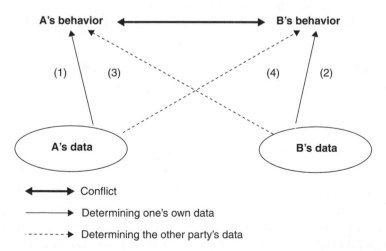

Figure 5.2   Adapting to the other party's data

Discussion

Once we thoroughly examine the preconditions for efficient power use, we discover that certain objective conflict data influence the efficiency of the parties to a significant extent. These data are called *conditions* and can be classified according to content.

Let us review the types of conditions present in a conflict with the help of information drawn from case studies 5.1 and 5.2:

(a) *Financial conditions*: Carl's initial and "final" financial conditions, the lack of valid opportunities to invest the US$210,000 (case study 5.2(a)), and the commercial value of his real estate, as well as Peter's additional burden at the time of the conflict with his competitor (case study 5.1).

(b) *Political conditions*: the fact that some clients wished to support Peter in the litigation (case study 5.1), Carl's decision to stand by his sick relative providing financial support (case study 5.2(b)), and Jessica's personal reasons for wanting to buy the apartment (case study 5.2(b)).

(c) *Time conditions*: Carl's time frame and urgent need to sell the apartment, the time during which Peter needed to be supported by his witnesses and the long time period set by the court to issue a verdict on the litigation.

(d) *Cultural conditions*: the way Jessica exploits Carl's need to sell the apartment, Peter's intention or unwillingness to agree with his competitor on ending the conflict, or even the very reaction of the competitor himself to this agreement. Part of this section also hinges on the rewards about to be given to Peter's supporters during the litigation period.

(e) *Legal conditions*: the evidence sought by the court to justify Peter.

(f) *Technical conditions*: the evidence of the guilt of Peter's discreditor, and the information Jessica received about the dire family and financial state that forced Carl to sell his property.

(g) *Complementary conditions*: Jessica's disappointment over her first negotiation with Carl and the way this disappointment influenced their final negotiations.

The entire cluster of conditions points out any obstacle or advantage concerning the use of power; all of which can prevent or give warning of the risk of inefficiency. The smaller the obstacles are when using power, the *more favorable* the conditions, and vice versa.

In other words, conditions are a "filter" for the kind of power we are going to invest, helping to determine the exact type and quantity of power needed to handle conflicts successfully.

Apart from this, efficiency is as highly dependent on the other party's conditions as on how the other party perceives both their own and our conditions.

However, any doubt as to whether these ideas lie in a *passive adaptation* to the existing conditions should be dismissed. On the contrary, the entire consideration aims at developing *active policies* to improve our conditions, and to change those of the other party, which will be discussed in Chapter 7 (pages 143–81). Before deepening these concepts, we will first define the content of each condition mentioned.

5.2 Types and content of conditions

Financial conditions

The content of financial conditions includes, for example: *financial needs, difficulties, dependencies, demands, expectations, plans.* As a rule, financial conditions are expressed in price, profit, cost, budget application, financial reports, and the like.

There is one question that must be answered in order to determine the influence of financial conditions in a conflict:

> In the event that the defined quantity of power is applied to influence the other party, how efficient could one be if the financial conditions were taken into consideration?

Case study 5.3 presents the influence of financial conditions during a negotiation.

Case study 5.3   William is performing audits for Cargo

William is a chartered auditor at Cargo; the company's managing director is Paul. While carrying out the audit, William ascertained some deficits in the Fixed Assets and Commodities of the business. Under normal circumstances, what William should do is let Paul know about the report before publishing it in compliance with the law. However, William is well aware of the fact that, if the audit goes public, Paul will be held accountable as being mainly responsible for the deficits.

Table 5.1 William, Paul and Cargo's deficits

Scenario 1	
William publishes the deficit report exactly as he set it up	
William: chartered auditor	*Paul: Cargo's managing director*
• Possible interruption of his collaboration with the company.	• The shareholders will consider him responsible.
• Possibility of not being compensated on time or fully by Cargo.	• Cargo will suffer financial consequences (i.e. a drop in share price, which will affect his career as well).
• Unfavorable career prospects as many CEOs of other companies will fear cooperation with him.	• There will be no future in his present relationships with Cargo.
	• Building a new career within other companies will be difficult.
Scenario 2	
William avoids publishing the deficits in the way he discovered them	
• He will face legal responsibilities in the event that the discrepancy is revealed between the company's true situation because of the deficits and the one he will present through his published report.	• He will keep his managerial position as a managing director of Cargo.
• He will suffer professional penalties and his professional license will be taken away.	• He will ensure a long-term collaboration with William, since it would be very risky to change auditor.

Table 5.1 exposes the way financial conditions influence both William's and Paul's behavior. According to the data in Table 5.1, the current financial conditions – as will those that occur in the future – trigger shifts in the entire negotiating process and the final outcome for each participant.

Political conditions

Political conditions include details resulting from the peculiar features of the parties and their relationships with others, such as:

- Undertakings, dependencies, alliances, means of support, conflicts with others.
- The way decisions are made and applied, and the ability to react and the speed with which that reaction takes place.
- Emotional intelligence.
- The way powers are distributed.
- Special abilities and weak points.

In order to determine how political conditions influence a conflict, we must answer to the following question:

> In the event that the defined quantity of power is applied to influence the other party, how efficient could one be if the political conditions were taken into consideration?

Case study 5.4 is built upon data that are present in political conditions:

Case study 5.4   John and Chris are involved in a long-lasting conflict

The multinational corporation John was working for transferred him from the head office in a Central European country to a subsidiary in country X to undertake the duties of a managing director. One of the basic criteria for choosing John is that he had previously lived and worked in country X for many years, which meant that he was thoroughly familiar with the language and the culture. As soon as John was assigned his new duties he met Chris, the general manager of an affiliated company. Chris was aged 58 years, meaning he was close to retirement, whereas John was aged 45.

1. The conflicts between the two men began immediately and lasted for seven years.
2. To settle their conflicts, the company used the services of a special mediator.
3. One of the most serious repercussions of their conflict was the fact that the entire staff had to work in disunity.

The known reasons for these conflicts were:

(a) Ten years ago, John had applied for the position of product manager at another company but had been rejected by Chris who, at the time, worked as a general manager for that particular company.
(b) When the subsidiary company was left with no managing director, Chris sought to be assigned to the position. He was somewhat taken aback when he realized that not only he had lost the position, but he was also going to be the subordinate of the man he had turned down 10 years earlier. Additional political elements of this case are presented in Table 5.2.

Table 5.2   John's and Chris' political data

John: managing director	Chris: general manager
Strong points – political elements	
• The company is favorable towards him.	✓ He is effective in terms of administrative tasks.
• The head office has no better solution for his position.	✓ He has great communication and creative qualities.
• He is young.	✓ His prestige within the professional field is indisputable.
• He shares the same mentality as the head-office representatives and speaks the language of the country where the subsidiary is located, which is crucial for the kind of product with which he deals.	✓ The head office fears that his experience might fall into the hands of competition.
Weak points	
• He is abstruse in his oral communication • He is extremely analytical to the point that he often "misses the forest for the tree" • He has less administrative qualification. • He is working centralized • He has disadvantages in decision-making.	✓ He is impulsive. ✓ His age is close to retirement. ✓ He is working centralized ✓ He is not aware of the latest administrative techniques. ✓ He often "misses the tree for the forest". ✓ He proves disadvantageous when setting up procedures.
Corporation policies after the start of the conflict	
John finds himself downgraded on the organization chart because of Chris's promotion to peer managing director.	Although Chris is promoted to peer managing director, his total income is decreased while more unfavorable terms are added to his retirement program.
Common benefits for John and Chris	
The success of the company adds prestige to their careers, and provides high incomes and acknowledgment from the head office.	

What is worth stressing at this point is that any political element regarding Chris as much as John, has favorably shaped during the conflict, despite the burden they have both caused for the company. Perhaps that was the main reason that kept the conflict going on for such a long time, causing trouble to the staff and the company's leadership.

Time conditions

As will be presented in detail in this section, time conditions usually refer to two topics:

(a) The most appropriate time to use power.
(b) For how long is it advisable to make use of powers in order to obtain desirable results.

Once again, it is necessary to answer the following question to ascertain the extent to which a conflict is influenced by time conditions:

> In the event that the defined quantity of power is applied
> to influence the other party, how efficient could one be
> if the time conditions were taken into consideration?

Usually, the timing of a conflict may favor or wrong one of the parties.

If we have the opportunity to choose when to engage in a conflict, we also ensure that its time schedule is planned. This is something we cannot do when time conditions are erratic (i.e. in unexpected crises). In these situations, the planning focuses on the redistribution of powers in the conflict fields until the conflict is over.

Mostly, in order to obtain desirable results it is necessary to invest powers over a larger time frame. So, before engaging in a conflict – and if the objective is to succeed – the required amount of time for the use of power

---

Example 5.1 Timing of a conflict

A union threatens to strike at a time when the business has to complete several orders; the strike would obviously cause large shortfalls. Vice versa: the business chooses to engage in conflicts with the union when going on a strike would be inefficient.

Example 5.2 Unavoidable failure

The success of a strike depends on how long the participants are prepared to keep it going until the employer gives way. If the strikers maintain the strike for only a short time, then the strike fails.

Example 5.3   Effects of unavoidable failure

In order for consumers to be satisfactorily influenced by advertising (i.e. to increase sales by 3 percent), new commercials must be broadcast for a specific period. If the company cannot afford the cost of the commercials over this time frame, they will not be able to influence consumers to the desirable degree, despite the money they have invested.

Example 5.4   Duration of power use

The efficiency of Company Y in public relations not only depends on the budget or the policies they apply, but also on how often they attempt to influence public opinion (using powers).

---

must have been already scheduled. If we cannot afford to use power, then failure is the unavoidable outcome.

What happens to a company interested in promoting its products is proportional to the situation in Example 5.2.

Therefore, another question arises: For how long should powers be invested to obtain the desired results?

Case study 5.5 helps determine certain aspects of time conditions.

Suddenly, new data were added to the conflict, thus making Bill change his behavior:

(a) The public insurance company represented by Bill became involved in a serious scandal for investing the contributions of insured members in dubious ways. As the scandal came to light, more unpleasant critics from polls expressing negative public opinion took the lead, causing trouble for the government.
(b) The fact that the government was pushed to declare premature elections could set public opinion; thus, the electorate would be more positive about the approval of Tom's project.

Table 5.3 overleaf shows how the negotiating data concerning Tom and Bill have ultimately been structured.

What is unquestionable is that Tom and Bill have been also influenced by the data outside the strict framework of time conditions. Nevertheless, the structuring of time conditions has eventually played a decisive role in

Table 5.3   Timing data in Tom's and Bill's negotiation

Tom	Bill
The parties' positions	
Selling the insulin along with the inhaling device and the related consumable goods.	Covering only the insulin-related expense for insured customers.
The initial parties' interests	
Increasing the company's long term profit by definitely selling the inhaling device and the related consumable goods to a huge market.	Avoiding the serious increase of the expense for the cure of diabetes (people suffering from diabetes represent a great percentage among insured customers).
Shift of data building the new time conditions	
1 Uncovering the scandal that caused issues to insured people: Bill must figure out an efficient solution for immediate customer satisfaction. 2 Unexpected pre-election campaign: The government must decide promptly about the benefits that they should grant to the electorate to gain a positive feedback.	
The final interests of the parties	
As mentioned before: Increasing the company's long term profit by definitely selling the inhaling device and the related consumable goods to a huge market.	1 Reducing the tensions created among the insured customers because of the scandal 2 Improving the image of the government towards the electorate by granting significant pre-election benefits.

Case study 5.5   Tom's and Bill's time conditions

Delta is a large multinational pharmaceutical corporation. Tom works as the managing director in one of its subsidiaries in a Mediterranean country. Delta has developed a form of insulin that can be inhaled to treat diabetes. Tom is negotiating with Bill, the representative of a huge public insurance company, for the insurance company's approval of the expense required to include provision of the product to insured customers free of charge.

1. Tom believes the public insurance company in question represents the most stable and profitable market in the entire country for that particular product.
2. Bill declines to approve this expense for two reasons:
   - because the cost is very high;
   - the cost does not relate exclusively to the insulin, but also to the inhaling device and the related dispensing mechanism as well.
3. The negotiations between Tom and Bill, who considered the product to be a "life style" commodity, were heading towards a dead-end.

the final outcome. If Tom and Bill had begun their negotiations after the national elections, the outcome of the conflict would have been different.

Cultural conditions

As a rule, those who take part in negotiation simulation exercises are the first to find out that the outcomes are different, although the exercise data are identical. A plausible explanation for having a variety of behaviors is that the parties are integrated into different cultural backgrounds. This is the case when one party:

- Aims at 50 and proceeds with a negotiation asking for 100; they gradually lower their requirement until the adversary agrees to give 50.
- Does not keep promises and tends to diverge from them.
- Has no inhibitions whatsoever for misleading their adversaries, while believing they are being smart and powerful in doing that.
- Culturally rejects the other party and rarely cooperates or agrees with others.
- Believes that certain negotiations must take place in specific venues, while the participants should respect a predetermined, unofficial protocol.
- Makes use of somewhat hard means.
- Is aggressive, bad-tempered, boisterous, lunatic, impulsive, unstable and over-the-edge.
- Aspires to personal profits, and even accepts third-party bribes, in order to afflict the benefits of their principal.
- Is pliant, scared, and insecure, and cannot put up with the pressure of other people's claims.

Regardless of the degree, cultural conditions mark the broader social context in which the other party is placed. When it comes to negotiations, we are more interested in the other party's personal cultural conditions when they might diverge considerably from the current conditions.

Here, also, the same question needs to be answered in order to define the components of culture conditions:

> In the event that the defined quantity of power is applied to influence the other party, how efficient could one be if the cultural conditions were taken into consideration?

Case study 5.6 shows part of this content.

Case study 5.6   Ellie and Alex's cultural profile

Ellie has been working for four years as a developer for Satellite, a programming company. Due to problems with the completion of a major project, the company decided to replace the previous project manager, assigning the task to Ellie. Ellie was confident that her promotion would also bring a raise in her salary: this not only did not happen, but Ellie also found herself with a lower salary compared with certain subordinates.

1. Every time she discussed the salary raise with her supervisor, Alex, he merely played for time and promised that the issue would be settled shortly.
2. Although the project was carried out satisfactorily, Ellie's salary remained low.
3. Ellie applied for employment with another company that offered her the desired salary.
4. When Ellie announced she would be quitting Satellite, Alex offered her a higher salary; the one for which she had been asking, in order to encourage her to stay.

Let us observe a more thorough presentation of these case data in Table 5.4.

Even the readers who can identify with Ellie's case will think of quite different outcomes, and that proves the influence of various cultural conditions in their "virtual" conflict with Alex. However, we have only determined three possible endings:

(a) She quits Satellite, even though her requests are finally fulfilled.
(b) She stays with Satellite, once her requests are completely fulfilled.
(c) She negotiates over her stay, demanding a higher salary and assurances regarding a future promotion.

There are additional, and perhaps more extreme, versions of Ellie's situation:

- Ellie bluffs about the fact that she found a new job, or that she is about to quit, in order to make Satellite give her the desired salary.

Table 5.4   The cultural conditions during Ellie's negotiation with Alex

Ellie	Alex
The parties' positions	
• Proportional paycheck raise to her promotion and the number of new responsibilities. • Higher salary than that of her subordinates.	• Putting off the raise until the project results are evident.
The parties' interests	
Fair treatment.	Keeping the cost low.
Behavior of the parties	

• Speaking often with Alex about improving her income.
• Applying to another company because of Alex's behavior.
	• Ignore Ellie's requests since:
	   – the market suffers a wider crisis while there are only few "healthy" businesses offering good jobs.
	   – Ellie had often expressed dissatisfaction about her salary in the past too, but never went on with the issue.

New data in the relationship	
She found a new job with the salary for which she kept asking Alex.	Invites Ellie to stay, giving her the desired salary, which equaled that offered by the other company.

- Ellie stops claiming a higher salary and starts taking advantage of her position as head of Satellite's project to gain personal profit from clients and/or company competitors.

So, what becomes clear from the entire exposition of facts is that predicting the other party's reaction to a conflict presupposes knowledge of their cultural conditions; the prediction is facilitated by the analysis of their past behaviors, even if these are various and divergent.

Legal conditions

Legal conditions are related to the way any third party handles a system of relationships and issues a compulsory decision on the final outcome of the conflict. The third party can be a court, arbitration or disciplinary committee, or any other such agency.

Despite the fact that we are within negotiating behaviors, negotiation researchers claim such obligatory decisions or appeals to similar institutions have nothing to do with negotiations. However, we firmly believe that legal conditions are part of negotiations, since the party that is favored uses them as a negotiating weapon. Accordingly, within the framework of legal conditions there is one important question:

> In the event that the defined quantity of power is applied to influence the other party, how efficient could one be if the legal conditions were taken into consideration?

When it comes to gaining benefits from legal conditions, efficiency presupposes an adequate mixture of other types of conditions, such as:

- *Financial conditions*: in the event of obtaining benefits from legal conditions, available financial means are required.
- *Political conditions*: when there is a need for legal support (i.e. witnesses).
- *Time conditions*: when a specific waiting period or time for the use of means must elapse before the final decision.
- *Cultural conditions*: when the members of institutions accept external interventions, or even when the application of their decisions diverges from their actual content.

Case study 5.7   Paul and his lawyer threaten Cristina

Cristina inherited a small printing unit from her father that employs 40 people. Unfortunately, the constant need to do overtime makes the unit shoulder an additional financial cost. To avoid this burden, Cristina put her father's tactics into practice: she agreed with her staff not to report the overtime to the National Institution for Social Security.

1. Overtime was being paid without issuing a receipt and the difference of the profit – meaning the contribution to the insurance organizations – was being shared between the business and the employees.
2. Paul was one of the workers that had agreed to follow this policy.
3. Five months after quitting the business, Paul lodged a suit against Cristina asking to be indemnified for last year's overtime, for which, he claimed, he had never been paid.
4. He also claimed that he had been forced to accept this agreement, otherwise he would have been fired.

Case study 5.7 presents a detailed version of case study 4.12, showing how certain aspects of legal conditions are covered.

For the lawsuit, Paul had the support of other employees who had worked at the business in the past, or who were about to leave. The total estimated time for the court to issue a decision is four years.

According to Cristina's information, Paul was prompted to proceed with the lawsuit by a local attorney who used to take commission on every case adjudged in the court.

Cristina's legal conditions were quite threatening due to the relative case law, though what she feared most was not indemnifying Paul with US$7,000 but, rather, paying the penalty imposed by the National Institution for Social Security as well as covering the court costs, which would double the expense.

In other words, it would be expected that more people who had recently quit or were going to do so would start filing an action and hoping for similar compensation. If this were the case, then Cristina's total financial expenses would amount to US$150,000.

As a last resort, Cristina also thought of closing down the printing unit because it would be impossible for her to afford to pay the amount of money that would be required. The influence of legal conditions on Paul's and Cristina's conflict appears on Table 5.5.

The data emerging from Table 5.5 show clearly the disadvantage Cristina is facing as far as legal conditions are concerned, which could negatively influence her behavior over the conflict. That is why she is going to do her best to keep the case out of the court room, not to mention that she will aim at discouraging other employees from suing her for damages. These developments would straighten out Paul and his lawyer during

Table 5.5 Legal conditions in Paul's and Cristina's conflict

Paul	Christina
The parties' positions	
• Win the litigation	• Avoid the US$7,000 indemnification penalty to Paul.
Real interests of the parties	
• For him: the US$7,000 profit. • For his attorney: financial benefits for handling Paul's and other people's cases.	• Ensure the survival of her business by avoiding indemnifying Paul, or other possible indemnities.
Behaviors of the parties	
• The trial's realization	• Avoid going on trial.

the forthcoming negotiations with Cristina. On the other hand, Cristina herself will negotiate more flexibly knowing that Paul and his lawyer may satisfy their interests without necessarily winning the lawsuit.

Technical conditions

This type of conditions includes the knowledge base and information that can intervene in a conflict. Technical conditions are favorable when one party can:

- Take advantage because of its special knowledge, information and technical supremacy.
- Have benefits from the other party's technical background.
- Resolve an issue with the other party to its advantage through technical opportunities.

So, following the same path as with the other types of conditions, to define the role that technicalities play in a conflict, one has to answer the question:

> In the event that the defined quality of power is applied to influence the other party, how efficient could one be considering the technical conditions?

Let us take a look at case study 5.8 to see how technical conditions have influenced the conflict between Mark and Brian:

Case study 5.8   Mark, Brian and the special paint coating

Mark represents Building, one of the largest national building contractors; Brian works for Tropho, a huge international food service company. The core of their conflict concerns a special fire-resistant paint used as a fire protection coating that is going to be used on a new three-story 40,000 sq m Tropho building. Construction has to be completed within 18 months. Immediately after signing the contracts, a conflict erupts concerning the lack of specification of the fire-resistant paint coating or its manufacturer. The only mention of the coating in the papers relate to quality specifications.

1. Brian insisted on using the paint that was manufactured by Painting, a worldwide established corporation. The product in question cost

four times more than a conventional paint produced by Colors (the product Mark suggested).

2. The fact that Colors was not yet an internationally established manufacturer, but only a newly-founded company gave Brian cause to mistrust its products.
3. Building had set the project budget based on the price list of Colors' products, so, if they accepted Brian's alternative, the budget would grow and the project would become unaffordable.
4. The conflict had already delayed the project by one month.

Table 5.6, describes the course of negotiations between the parties and how they were influenced by technical conditions:

Table 5.6   The course of negotiations between Mark and Brian

Mark (Building)	Brian (Tropho)
The parties' positions	
Use an alternative material for the fire-resistant paint produced by Colors (within the required standards).	Use Painting's material, which is a worldwide established brand of fire-resistant paints.
The parties' interests	
The material should comply with: • the agreed standards. • the budget and cost schedule of Building	The material should guarantee the protection of the construction against fire (as would be the case with Painting's product)
Time and legal data	
The duration of the construction period has been agreed at 18 months and there will be penalties for delays. There has already been a one-month delay, for which Mark might be held responsible but this is not definite.	
Actions of the parties (1)	
Mark ensures the expert opinion of an independent national-level control company to prove that the fire-resistant paint products of Painting and Colors are equally good.	Brian is not convinced of the reliability of this expert and rejects the proof.
Actions of the parties (2)	
Mark obtains the written certification of Painting about the three different layers of the fire-resistant paint. If the first layer is realized with Painting's product and the other two layers with Colors' materials, the result will be perfectly compatible with the agreed standards set between Mark and Brian.	Brian accepts the certification and agrees to proceed with the three-layer coat suggested by Painting.

To sum up, the conflict was ultimately resolved due to the latest technical conditions, which evolved to satisfy the interests of the parties. Despite their special role in the entire process, more types of conditions were involved that should not to be omitted:

(a) *Legal conditions*: The vague contract content concerning the paint's specifications was probably planned on purpose by Mark; and perhaps even the inability to blame Mark for the delayed start of the works.
(b) *Time conditions*: The necessary period for completing the project and the one-month delay to the start of construction.
(c) *Cultural conditions*: Tropho mistrusted the certification of the national independent quality control company.
(d) *Political conditions*: Mark obtained the support of the national independent quality control company and, eventually, managed to convince Painting as well.
(e) *Financial conditions*: Mark believed Painting's material was expensive in comparison with that of Colors. The fact that Painting approved Colors' material is probably connected to the balance of Painting's profits.

Complementary conditions

Unlike their name, complementary conditions are not any less significant than other types of conditions. The analysis of case study 5.9 and Table 5.7 helps support this concept.

Case study 5.9   Joan, Mary, and 70 purchase managers

Joan is about to make a presentation of a new line of company products to 70 purchase managers from different large client companies or to potential clients. The presentation will take place in a central hotel. The feedback at the end of the work will strongly determine the emergence of the product in the market, which is a decisive element in its overall success. Three days before the presentation, Joan assigns the final check of the material and the procedures to Mary, her trusted assistant. The following day, Mary reports back to Joan all the possible risks of the event failing related to complementary conditions. It was at that point that Joan realized that she had been ignoring them, convinced that everything was under control.

Table 5.7   Joan's unfavorable complementary conditions

Venue issue
The chosen venue was a long, narrow room that would inhibit the visual contact of the speaker with the participants sitting beyond the fifth row.

Consequences
(a) It would be impossible for Joan to see what impression her presentation made on the participants sitting beyond the eighth row, and that would also prevent adapting her presentation to their needs.
(b) The ones sitting beyond the eighth row would feel cut off, given they would lack a proper visual contact with the multimedia material.

Mary's suggestion
Find a room with a more appropriate shape.

Incompatibility of technical means
Joan's equipment was incompatible with that of the room. To resolve the issue, the first 15 minutes of the presentation would be spent troubleshooting the equipment, thus delaying the whole procedure.

Consequences
(a) Joan would start feeling nervous and insecure at the sight of the seated audience waiting for the busy technicians to finish their work.
(b) The clients would complain about the delay and criticize both Joan's professionalism and the organization of the event. Eventually, the audience would start talking about other topics and lose interest in the forthcoming presentation.

Mary's suggestion
Troubleshoot the technical issue before the very beginning of the presentation.

Ambient temperature
The estimated ground temperature that day would be 37°C, and the room's air-conditioning system would not be able to meet the needs for so many people.

Consequences
(a) Soon after the beginning of the presentation, the heat would make Joan feel uncomfortable while standing and moving back and forth in the room. Her discomfort would become evident to every person present in the room.
(b) The participants would start becoming uncomfortable in the overheated room, so they would have difficulty in paying full attention to the presentation.

Mary's suggestion
Pick a room with a powerful air-conditioning system.

The lunch
Thanks to the special hotel prices, the lunch preceding the presentation was planned to be plentiful. That, combined with the heat, would make it hard for participants to focus on Joan's work.

Consequences
Soon after the introduction of the presentation, the participants would begin to feel heavy and tired, and the presentation itself would eventually become boring.

Mary's suggestion
Replace the existing menu with a lighter one, even at the same cost. As for Joan, she would only be formally present at the lunch.

(continued)

Table 5.7   Continued

Inconvenience-disorientation circumstances
The day of the presentation the hotel had arranged to carry out some works on the upper floor. The works would go on during the entire presentation, causing noise. In addition to this, through the large window of the room the participants would be distracted by the sight of hotel guests passing by.

Consequences
These external factors would worsen Joan's contact with the clients; some of them would be irritated by the constant noise, whereas others would divert their attention towards the distracting guests.

Mary's suggestion
Avoid having distractions in the room to allow participants to focus on the content of the meeting.

The sequence of the presented topics
Joan had, indeed, thought of a very logical presentation sequence for the topics; however, in Mary's opinion it had to be revised because it started with "difficult" topics, such as the company's invoice policy.

Consequences
The clients would react to Joan's approach and start behaving defensively towards her arguments, thinking she was aiming at raising the prices of products.

Mary's suggestion
Joan should avoid mentioning "delicate" topics, such as prices, as this could cause the participants anxiety or doubt. It would be better to discuss such matters in private with each client individually, rather than face them all together.

Joan's physical condition
During the last days, Joan has not been feeling very well because of the preparation for the presentation. On the morning of the presentation, Joan had arranged to meet with some company representatives coming from abroad.

Consequences
Her bad physical condition over the last few days would add to her tiredness at the morning meeting and decrease her energy levels and the quality of her presentation.

Mary's suggestion
Joan should postpone the morning meeting and avoid taking on additional burdens on the day of the presentation.

Table 5.7 presents the facts showing that complementary conditions, together with other types of conditions, play a significant role in reaching total efficiency. To avoid complications of incompatibility from this type of condition, it is crucial to find an answer to the next question:

> In the event that the defined quantity of power is applied to influence the other party, how efficient could one be considering the complementary conditions?

5.3 Conditions: characterization and measurements

What becomes clear from the preceding analysis is that, in a conflict, only one kind of condition prevails; the others appear simultaneously but are ancillary.

Prevailing and ancillary conditions

When there are more types of conditions in a conflict, it is easier to ascertain their degrees of influence. Therefore, according to those degrees of influence, conditions are divided into two categories: *prevailing* and *ancillary*. Prevailing conditions are crucial to leading the parties to efficiency; ancillary conditions are of secondary significance.

Nevertheless, the dynamics of a conflict might change the nature of the prevailing conditions for a variety of reasons (i.e. after agreement has been reached between the two parties, or due to accidental events, or even after applying a particular strategy). This is the case when one party believes that it will receive no benefits from the prevailing conditions, and so manages to reduce the other party's resistance, replacing the former prevailing conditions with conditions it considers to be more appropriate.

If the shift is due to accidental events, then the parties behave according to whether they consider the new type of conditions profitable or not. If the shift in conditions is due to accidental events, the parties accept matters and try to preserve the agreement. If the shift is due to one of the parties applying a particular strategy, the other party will aim at replacing disadvantageous prevailing conditions.

As far as ancillary conditions are concerned, people may think that, because of their limited significance, they are entirely trivial. However, this estimation is wrong: overlooking ancillary conditions could decrease or eliminate any efficiency whatsoever.

Example 5.5   Relevant ancillary conditions

In competition where the award of a contract goes to the lowest bidder, the prevailing conditions are technical in terms of the software supply. However, in order to win the contract there is a need for a trustworthy third party who will confirm one's reliability.

> ## Example 5.6   Irrelevant ancillary conditions
>
> The technical conditions of the competition are not particularly urgent; consequently they can be fulfilled almost by any candidate supplier. That is why the final selection mainly depends on how many committee members are familiar with the candidate suppliers.

If there is no such third-party support – *political conditions* – one's competition bid will probably be turned down. Let us reverse this example to shift the nature of conditions.

Despite the fact that, in this example, political conditions prevail, inability to cope with the technical conditions, which are ancillary, would lead to failure.

Mix of conditions

To sum up, since every conflict shows the co-existence of various kinds of conditions with different degrees of influence, we take it for granted that every conflict contains a mix of *conditions* affecting the final conflict result, according to its synthesis.

This mix determines the installments of the kinds of power reserves, which, according to the conditions, are indispensable for achieving the desired efficiency. In other words, the first step for predicting our conflict efficiency is to determine the extent to which our powers are quantitatively and qualitatively compatible with the mix of conditions. This will allow us to understand whether the available power mixture is favorable or not.

If the available power mixture is favorable, the target would be to exploit the mixture in the best way possible. If the available power mixture is unfavorable, it is preferable to avoid the conflict completely. Not engaging in the conflict is intended to adapt first the powers in the combination data, or even to change the mix as though adjusting the available powers. Alternatively, more ways of adapting the powers to the current mix of conditions are sought.

The other parties are thinking in the same way; thus, their intentions and practices can be predicted, since they depend on whether the mix of their conditions favors them or not.

According to this example, the financial conditions that were prevailing initially were not profitable to property owners. That is why they changed the situation with the help of political conditions. However, as time passes

---

Example 5.7   Exploiting the mix

The commercial value of real estate in a specific area has leapt from US$2,500 per sq m to US$4,000. The prices increased immediately after the property owners agreed not to sell for less than US$4,000 per sq m. The ability to maintain the high prices will depend on whether all the owners will be able to stick to the agreement in the foreseeable future.

---

time conditions become progressively more significant (if the estates remain unsold at US$4,000 per sq m, there is a greater probability that, after a while, the owners will not keep to the agreement because of their financial difficulties). Consequently, if someone is interested in purchasing a piece of real estate property in that area but will not agree to the price of US$4,000 per sq m, they must wait until the agreement between owners collapses, perhaps after talking other potential buyers out of paying this high price.

Measuring obstacles on the way to efficiency

We are all aware how favorable conditions aid efficiency and unfavorable conditions put it in jeopardy. This is a useful piece of information when it comes to determining the extent to which conditions help us achieve our goals.

Of course, as mentioned, efficiency does not depend exclusively on our own conditions but also on the other party's ability to be efficient. This is a good reason why we should measure the degree of positive or negative influence of conditions on the other party. Measurements will be of great help in understanding the way the other party takes advantage of their profitable conditions while, at the same time, they try to cover or mislead us regarding their adverse conditions.

Table 5.8 records and measures the corresponding obstacles and requirements related to the conditions of player A and player B within a conflict.

The data in Table 5.8 are only hypothetical, but nonetheless help in discussing the topic. The columns show all types of conditions as previously analyzed: financial, political, time, cultural, legal, technical and complementary. At the bottom of each column, there is a reference to the degree of influence of the corresponding condition in the conflict, for which a scale has been used ranging from 0 (no influence) to 5 (maximum influence). Based on the data in Table 5.8, the prevailing conditions in the conflict between A and B are political, with a maximum influence (5). The remaining

Table 5.8 Obstacles to A's and B's efficiency

Influence of conditions / Obstacles within conditions	Financial conditions (3) Large influence	Political conditions (5) Maximum influence	Time conditions (4) Very large influence	Cultural conditions (1) Small influence	Legal conditions (1) Small influence	Technical conditions (3) Large Influence	Complementary conditions (1) Small influence
0 = prohibitive							
1 = large							A B
2 = several	B	B	A			B	
3 = few				A B	B	A	
4 = very few		A	B		A		
5 = none	A						

———— Obstacles of player A.

············ Obstacles of player B.

conditions affect the conflict to various degrees, although time conditions reach a peak of 4 (very large influence). Next come the financial and technical conditions (3); and, finally, the legal and complementary conditions, with a minimum degree of influence (1).

Once these measurements have been made, we need to find out whether A and B are capable of fulfilling these conditions (i.e. how easy it is for them to use powers). For this purpose, we use the same scale, ranging from prohibitive conditions (0) to conditions that do not constitute an obstacle to any player for the use of power (5).

The volume of obstacles is depicted by the lines in Table 5.8: the steady line records A's obstacles and the dotted line exhibits B's problems. This table helps us ascertain the extent to which the two players are favored or hampered by conflict conditions.

It is therefore quite obvious when it comes to the political conditions, which are crucial to the particular conflict between players A and B (5), that A has very few obstacles (4) and takes the lead over B who has a few impediments (3). Conversely, in terms of time conditions, which also affect the conflict considerably (4), A faces large obstacles, while B who is ahead faces none (5). And again, with regard to financial conditions bringing large shifts to the conflict (3), A holds a better position because there are no obstacles whatsoever (5), whereas B has to deal with several (2). As far as technical conditions are concerned, both parties have obstacles to deal with, even though A only has a few (3) and B has several (2). Finally, with regard to cultural, legal and complementary conditions, these conditions exercise little influence on the conflict (1). The situation is mixed: cultural conditions see B a little ahead (4) compared with A (3); with regard to legal conditions, A has no obstacles at all (5), whereas B has a few (2); regarding complementary conditions, the two adversaries are equal and face no impediments (5).

To sum up, if we take Table 5.8 as a starting point, we can develop policies for the preservation and improvement of our efficiency. These policies will be examined in the following sections.

5.4 Efficiency: preservation and improvement

As soon as the conflict data trigger questions within the framework of conditions, we are led to seek new policies in order to improve them. Such policies are:

- Achieving synergies.

- Avoiding obstacles.
- Expanding conditions.
- Creating a more beneficial mix of conditions.

Achieving synergies through conditions: 2 + 2 = 5

At this stage, synergies are achieved when:

- Problems arising from dire conditions are resolved with minimum means.
- Favorable conditions are exploited in the best way possible.

Resolving problems using minimum means and conditions that are favorable lead us to *positive synergies* (2 + 2 = 5), creating advantageous outcomes exceeding any expectation in terms of the available conditions. Conversely, the presence of dire and unfavorable conditions causes *negative synergies* (2 + 2 = 3), leading us to shortfalls.

According to Table 5.8, player A has no obstacles in financial conditions (5); however, with regard to time conditions their impediments are considerable (1). That is why A could use the available financial means on B who is having significant problems in the financial field (2), to be later favored by B in terms of time conditions. Player A finally accomplishes synergy when the value of the financial means, used to be facilitated by B in terms of time conditions, is smaller than the total profit value gained because of this facilitation.

If A considers the achievement of positive synergy through B less profitable, A will aim at achieving the positive synergy with whomsoever else is capable of resolving the issue of time conditions more efficiently. The following examples show additional cases of synergy where A achieves set goals towards B by using:

- Fewer evolved technical means than are immediately available. As a result, A saves more sophisticated means for a future interaction with B.
- Fewer political resources than are readily available, after convincing B that the opposite is the case.
- Much less time than is required under normal circumstances, because they use some third party (political conditions) to influence B, or even use technical conditions to influence more players simultaneously (i.e. teleconferences).

To achieve synergies, it is necessary either to combine conditions successfully or to substitute unusable powers (powers that cannot be invested because of adverse conditions) with other types of power that the conditions will favor.

Avoiding obstacles to achieve efficiency

Often, we feel confident that we will finally reach the desired result as conditions assure us of our supremacy over the other party. However, despite this supremacy it is possible that we might fail due to a variety of factors (e.g. the attainable level of negotiation, the insufficiency in power of the stronger party, and the excessive weakness of the other party).

Obstacle 1: the attainable level of negotiation

The stronger party often fails to shift the behavior of the weaker party because they might be equally efficient. For example, in a negotiation A owns 100 power units and B only 50. We could suppose that A will ultimately predominate over B but this does not happen, because the structure of the negotiating conditions requires only 50 power units, which both players can afford.

Based on Table 5.8, we locate the general impediment on legal conditions, where A is stronger (5) than B (2). Even though A predominates, they cannot gain proportionally large benefits because legal conditions have only a low-level influence on the conflict (1). Therefore, despite the difficulties, player B could have a chance to rise to the occasion as well as A.

If A intends to obtain profits that are proportional to their supremacy in legal conditions, A must increase the degree of influence of those conditions in the entire engagement, so that B will not be able to compensate.

Example 5.8   Avoiding obstacles (1)

A salesman in an audio equipment store is trying to convince a customer to purchase a pair of expensive speakers. Although the salesman has a broad knowledge of sound systems, he fails to convince the customer because the customer's limited knowledge of speakers is sufficient to allow him work out that the sound effect will not be compatible with the high price of the speakers.

Example 5.9   Avoiding obstacles (2)

The salesman fails to convince the customer to purchase the expensive speakers because he does not have the answer to the customer's additional questions on product specifications. The salesman's inability to answer these questions ultimately disappoints the customer, who starts doubting the salesman's expertise.

Obstacle 2: the power insufficiency of the stronger party

This obstacle arises when it is impossible to change the other party's behavior in any way whatsoever due to the lack of sufficient powers. In other words, this occurs if A has 100 power units and B has 50 but, despite any prediction of A's success, A does not manage to prevail because they do not have in stock the indispensable extra reserves (e.g. 120 units of powers).

Example 5.9 augments Example 5.8.

Needless to say, insufficiency might also occur within political conditions: the data of Table 5.8 show A ahead (4) of B (3), but A still cannot influence B as they lack the maximum influence level (5). To reach this level, A must expand his powers for achieving the highest level (5), while at the same time keeping B at their current level (3).

Obstacle 3: the excessive weakness of the other party

As a rule, the greater the discrepancy of power reserves between the parties, the more advantageous the position of the stronger player is in the conflict. Against all odds, in order to exercise influence we need to strengthen the other party. If we fail to do so, our supremacy turns to a minus; for example, A has 100 power units but cannot influence B, who has only 50. In this case, B would need more than only 50 units (i.e. 75) to be influenced.

Example 5.10 augments Example 5.9.

Referring quickly to Table 5.8, the obstacle of the other party's weakness would be located within financial conditions, where A has no difficulty at all in responding to circumstances (5). Conversely, player B is dealing with serious financial issues (2). Overall, if A wishes to achieve financial cooperation with B, he should support B at a financial level in order to bring B closer, which ultimately benefits A.

Example 5.10   Avoiding obstacles (3)

The salesman cannot convince the customer because the customer is unable to understand the details of the speakers' advantages and specifications (such as their material, sensitivity impedance, flexibility, engineering, measured performance). The customer needs a much higher level of technical knowledge than he currently has to decode the information provided by the salesman.

Expanding conditions

We often believe that present conditions are favorable, although this does not keep us from predicting their adverse course: that is why expanding conditions ensures our future efficiency. Similar scenarios are characteristic in long-term relationships (i.e. with customers, suppliers, colleagues) and seldom occur in short-term relationships (i.e. the purchase of real estate).

These developments mean that A's services will no longer be indispensable to the company for at least the next two years – until such time as it is necessary to sign a new collective agreement with the union, or until the company finally stays with its initial plan to apply the new performance appraisal system. To avoid such a development – which could eventually lead the company to decide it no longer requires A's services – A seeks ways to preserve his consultancy with the company. Put simply, A tries to expand conditions by:

(a) Convincing the company and the union not to sign the two-year collective agreement that would cut A off from the company. Furthermore, A strives to make them approve the new performance appraisal system

---

Example 5.11   Expanding conditions

A is a company consultant specialized in matters relating to labor law. More specifically, he was assigned issues regarding the company's union collective bargaining, and the development and application of a new staff performance appraisal system. At some point, A learns that the company intends to sign a two-year collective labor agreement with the union. In addition to this, the company is starting to have second thoughts about the current application of a new performance appraisal system.

---

as a pilot program with an intention to expand it in the future, always with regard to the results and course of conditions. These are the "tools" used by A to buy some time until he finds a new reason for the company to require his consultancy services. His success will depend on the political conditions (i.e. the relationships with the company executives who make the decision regarding hiring external consultants).

(b) Making the company realize that a "new" necessity would make A indispensable to the management (collaboration renewal). If he manages to achieve that, then during this new consultancy A will try to change the company's mind about not introducing the new performance appraisal system. Simultaneously, he makes sure that the new consultancy lasts at least two years, so as to continue to be a company consultant until the next collective negotiations with the union begin. A's success depends, as before, on political and technical conditions: A must prove himself to be competent in perceiving and covering the company's needs.

(c) Preserving and further improving interpersonal relationships with company executives (those that make the decisions regarding external consultants), having as main goal to be assigned a new project. The goal is to keep the consultancy going forward in order to ensure future cooperation.

At this point, whether these tactics will be successful depends as much on the extent to which various conditions influence A's negotiations with the company as they do the obstacles A must face in those conditions.

Of course, in the above three strategies A must avoid being affected by financial conditions that would jeopardize the company's approval of these suggestions (i.e. the rejection of any kind of consultancy because of the inadequate cover of his financial demands).

Shaping the mix of conditions

A's strategies are mainly projected towards adaptation to the boosting or replacing of conditions, or to conditions' evidence. Besides these tactics, there are others aimed either at changing the entire mix of conditions by adding a further condition, or at recreating the mixture from scratch.

According to Table 5.8, given that A is not facilitated by the existing mix of conditions in terms of his relationship with B, A may try to replace it. The new mix should fully exploit A's favorable conditions, while removing B's advantages. So, A makes sure that financial and legal conditions are

---

Example 5.12   Shaping the mix of conditions

A ascertains that political and time conditions greatly influence the outcome of business competition in which the award will go to the highest bidder. A is greatly disadvantaged in these kinds of conditions, but is in the lead regarding financial and legal conditions. As a result, A tries to restrict the field of activity in political and time conditions and, at the same time, increases the influence of financial and legal conditions within the competition. The change puts A ahead of any competitor with insufficient powers in those conditions.

---

decisive in the new mix (5), whereas time conditions exercise the minimum degree of influence. Seemingly, that would remove any advantage from B and benefit A.

In order to be stable, new relationships require legal regulation, binding agreements or even inflexible procedures with regard to amendment – with the aid of collateral interests – that would cause serious impediments to achieving a revision. New relationships are supported by internal rules, systems of individual or collective labor agreements, cooperation agreements, and whatever might bind the participants to adopt a specific behavior protocol.

5.5 Summary

Efficiency depends on the ability to employ *sufficient* and *compatible* powers in a conflict engagement. To achieve this, we trace back the prevailing conditions of the conflict: financial, political, time, cultural, legal, technical and complementary. Determining these conditions would be sufficient to scan efficiency, if there were only one predominant type of condition in each case. Since, though, this seldom occurs, every conflict is enriched by more types of conditions.

At this point, it has been necessary to define the so-called *mix of conditions*. In every mix there is a prevailing type of condition, while the other types of condition co-exist with different degrees of influence in the conflict episode. Consequently, the mix of conditions says a great deal about the sufficiency and compatibility levels of the powers the conflict requires.

This is a way of predicting the efficiency of the parties, and can be achieved by comparing the significance of each condition within the mix with the ability of each party to respond appropriately to the corresponding type of condition.

Thus, we finally find out in which conditions we should improve ourselves, through the development of corresponding policies and practices.

Such policies and practices aspire either to make the best use of powers – by achieving synergies and avoiding obstacles in order to reach efficiency and expand the range of conditions, or to shape a more favorable mix of conditions due to prompt actions (which will be discussed later).

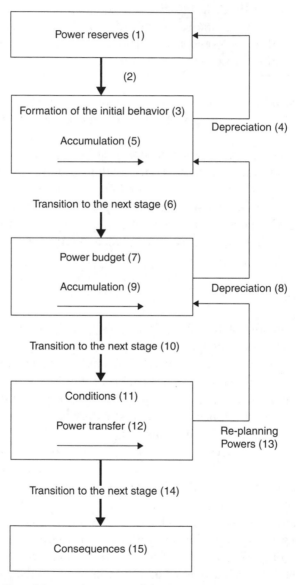

Figure 5.3   Transition to the stage of the consequences

Let us take a look at the following conclusion:

> The more favorable the conditions, the more
> efficient we can be within a conflict and the more
> active our presence is in it, and vice versa.

5.6 Moving on to the next stage

As soon as the stage regarding conditions is completed, a variety of behaviors emerges. These behaviors are presented in Figure 5.3, which augments Figure 4.6. The first action to be recorded at this stage is the transfer of powers from excessive fields to insufficient fields (12). If the power migration does not eventually lead to the reinforcement of insufficient fields, then we return (13) to the preceding stage (7) in order to take action in fields that are under accumulation (9), which leads to re-planning the use of our powers within our conflict fields. The same happens when the powers are excessive (i.e. because of positive synergies or due to an unexpected withdrawal of the adversary from a conflict, or their reduced participation in it).

Once these actions are undertaken, we pass (14) to the stage of consequences (15), where we examine the repercussions of our alternative behaviors. This is essential, as even efficient behaviors may prove to be disadvantageous for the reasons illustrated in Chapter 6.

CHAPTER 6

Evaluation of consequences

An efficient negotiation strategy does not always ensure its effectiveness. For this reason, it is important to assess the consequences concerning the costs, profits, positive and negative influences and their duration that may follow our actions. This assessment is based on the definition of the consequences for each of the stages previously discussed (power reserves, formation of initial behavior, power budget and conditions). As yet, the picture is not complete until we consider the other party's behavior: this leads to the development of the concept of "predictable behaviors".

The preceding stage proved that efficiency can be overcome by a proper background of favorable conditions. Needless to say, such an optimistic point of view could make anyone move towards the realization of plans without considering the hidden risks. The case studies that follow help us understand this concept:

Case study 6.1   Nick, his collaborators and the proposal to Jim

(a) Nick, his collaborators and Jim

Nick and his collaborators have worked hard to submit a cooperation proposal to the company Jim represents. The US$1,000,000 bonus that will be paid in the event that the proposal is approved will guarantee the survival of Nick's work group for at least the next two years.

(b) Nick and the unknown driver

While driving to the meeting, the traffic lights turn red and Nick brings his car to a halt. Across the street, 100 feet away, there is a parked patrol car. While waiting for the traffic lights to turn green, he realizes that the driver of the adjacent vehicle is jeering at him, but he has absolutely no clue what the fuss is about.

1. Nick does not react to the jeering because his mind is on the meeting.
2. His passive behavior infuriates the other driver, who gets out of the car and begins to move towards him.
3. The stranger's appearance gives Nick the impression that he should be concerned that someone wishes to start a fight with him.
4. At the very moment the driver approaches Nick's car, the traffic lights turn green.

Nick hopes for the best, and Jim's interest in the collaboration project overcomes any pressure exercised by the team's competitors. Despite any positive approach, though, there is no certainty whatsoever regarding the final decision. Nick knows that similar agreements have been cancelled in the past within a very short time before they were due to be signed. Let us observe the parameters that Nick planned so carefully in advance to achieve maximum results:

- The venue, the day, the time, and the desired duration of the meeting (in accordance with Jim's preference).
- The communication climate during the preliminary discussions (before starting the negotiations over the terms and the nature of their collaboration).
- The partner who will assist him during the meeting, and their mode of intervention.
- The dress code.
- The sequence of the topics to be presented and their exact content.
- The means by which to provide answers to Jim's questions or observations.
- The amendments Jim could request on Nick's suggestions, and so on.

Nick has arranged to arrive at the location of the meeting 15 minutes before the beginning of the session. His partner will be waiting for him outside the building.

No matter how dramatic the scenario of case study 6.1(b) might sound, if Nick chooses to stay there and not drive away, he has at least two options with which to be efficient in his conflict with the unknown driver:

(a) Face the unknown driver personally.
(b) Ask the police for their intervention.

However, regardless of Nick's choice, the outcome will be the same. If he faces the unknown driver personally, the policemen will intervene in a few minutes; if Nick asks the police for their intervention, they will respond to his call. All parties will then be escorted to the nearest police station to be taken to account.

Consequently, both tactics will make Nick efficient in tackling the aggressiveness of the unknown driver but will have negative repercussions. Either his late arrival at the meeting or his canceling the appointment with Jim could put his aspirations at risk. Jim may think that Nick is unprofessional for not arriving at the meeting, or, if Jim found out why Nick did not attend the meeting, he may believe that Nick is bad-tempered or immature.

Even if nothing happened at all, there is a high probability that a competitor would in the meantime arrange to make a deal with Jim and steal the opportunity from Nick's hands. To avoid any undesirable consequences, Jim would need to have experienced a similar traumatic episode; this could lead him to sympathize with Nick and identify with him. But to what extent is that probable; and would it be worth Nick taking the risk?

Overall, the coercive time conditions hardly allow Nick to analyze the data to understand that it would be better for him not to engage in a conflict, despite his perception that he could deal with it efficiently. However, even if he had all the time available to choose the most appropriate reaction, he should undergo the following decision-making conflict handling process.

6.1 The process of selecting conflict-handling strategies

Usually, there are more ways in which to handle a conflict; we finally select the most beneficial method in accordance with the process described in Figure 6.1.

Based on this figure, the main objective is to choose the best way possible to handle our conflict (2), one that *maximizes the total profit* (1). To achieve something like this, we have to discover:

- The kinds of benefits and deficits within a specific choice, given any selection that includes a number of pros and cons expressed throughout the criteria that determine the consequences (3).
- The content and the costs of benefits and deficits, which can be determined as soon as we define the resources of the consequences (4).
- The expected reactions (i.e. the behavior of the other party (5)), which can extend our benefits and deficits according to the choices we make to handle the conflict.

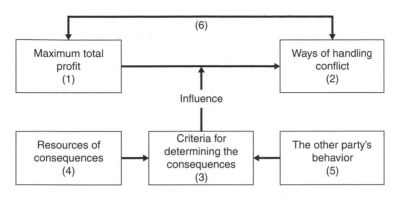

Figure 6.1   The conflict-handling selection process

At this point, it is important to mention that we may be led to change what we have chosen (6) in the event that we predict that a specific strategy will not result in a desired outcome due to the shift of data (i.e. the behavior of the other party).

6.2 Criteria for determining the consequences

To determine the total cost of profit, we often sum up benefits and deficits as a whole. Let us check the next two ways to handle a conflict:

(a) The first party gives 100 units of benefit and produces 60 units of deficit. The total profit is: 40.
(b) The second party gives 80 units of benefit and 20 units of deficit. Total profit: 60.

Obviously, scenario (b) provides a greater profit altogether when compared with scenario (a).

Thus, the formula used to estimate the total profit is relatively elementary, as it expresses both benefits and deficits in simple monetary units. The criteria for calculating these types of results are: *cost, damages, profit*.

However, a conflict is constantly enriched with additional positive and negative values that cannot possibly be converted to money units, in spite of their strong influence on benefits (i.e. prestige, defamation, volume of changes, extension of influence, risk reduction).

The content of these consequences is varied and can be conveyed in money units only in an indirect way; that is why, in order to define them, we use the criteria of *positive and negative influences*.

The effect of similar influences lasts for a specific time period so, when they have a different duration, they shift the total sum of consequences proportionally. For example, one choice may create a negative influence of US$100 for the next three months; a different choice may create a negative influence of US$50 every three months for the next 12 months. As a result, the list of criteria becomes extended with the addition of another consideration: *the duration of the negative and positive influences*.

Cost and damages

Cost and damages are the solid part of a conflict engagement that facilitate the interpretation and prediction of the parties' behaviors.

Besides the *cost* because of the conflict's manifestation, there are two more conflict costs: *the protraction cost* and *the expiry cost*. Example 6.2 augments Example 6.1.

The protraction cost means the company has to shoulder further losses, while the strikers will suffer the reduced or zero income for the entire duration of the strike.

This is also the case with regard to the expiry cost of the conflict: In order for the strike to be called, the company will have to compensate the strikers with a larger amount of money compared with what the company would have paid to its employees before the strike. Let us imagine a plausible scenario.

Example 6.1   Cost and damages (1)

For example, the calling of a strike has a cost the strikers as much as for the company. The company's cost arises from the losses of its profit because the work was called to a halt; the strikers lose their corresponding income because of the strike.

Example 6.2   Costs and damages (2)

If the strike continues, then the duration of the strike produces the cost of its protraction.

Example 6.3   Costs and damages (3)

Before the strike, the company had planned to spend US$100,000 to raise the level of the employees' salaries. Due to the pressure exercised by the strikers, the company is obliged to pay US$130,000. In this case, the expiry cost for the company amounts to US$30,000.

Example 6.4   Costs and damages (4)

If each striker calls the strike to achieve a raise in their salary by US$80 but the employer agrees to pay only US$50 more, then the expiry cost of the conflict for every striker is up to US$30 per month.

Proportionally, the same pattern applies to estimating the expiry cost of the conflict to the strikers (Example 6.4).

There are many occasions when court costs – the financial rewards to third parties aimed at helping one of the original parties to the lawsuit – and the damages (i.e. wearing of products or equipment, and so forth) that result from a conflict reach a sum equivalent to the total cost of the legal engagement.

The volume of each cost and damage influences the behavior of the parties. This means that, if the conflict's protraction cost is greater than its expiry cost, then it is preferable to end it, and vice versa (if the conflict's protraction cost is less than its expiry cost, then it is more profitable to protract the conflict instead of ending it).

If, in case study 6.1, Nick decides to face the unknown driver, his damage would start with US$1,000,000 which is the amount that his team would earn with the approval of the proposal. In addition to this, if the project is turned down and his team cannot continue, he will also lose the incomes that would have been achieved had his team continued to function. Finally, if the episode with the unknown driver reached the courts, he would probably also have to bear the corresponding costs.

Profit

What happens often is mistaking a conflict for a mere event full of costs and damages, but this is wrong. A conflict has the potential to yield profit resulting from its realization, protraction and expiry.

Example 6.5   Profit

Some production floor employees decide to call a strike. What they ignore is that the company has stockpiled sufficient products to supply customers for the next two months. The company has therefore managed to make a saving of the value of wages it did not pay to its employees while they were on strike. Moreover, the company also saved the cost of keeping the products in stock, while production would continue as usual in the event that the strike was not called. These data show that the company can afford the strike for some considerable time. However, the strikers decide to end the strike because they cannot afford its protraction cost. The end of the strike ultimately causes the employees to agree to a smaller raise in wages compared with that planned by the company before the beginning of the strike. The company had originally intended to pay US$100,000 on a monthly basis to raise the employee's salaries but eventually gives US$80,000.

Against all odds, by the end of the conflict the company has a clear profit resulting from the realization, protraction and expiry of the conflict. The profit is US$20,000 on a monthly basis, which adds to the saving of the labor cost of the strikers and the expenses for keeping the additional goods in stock.

To sum up, the kind of profit we earn from a conflict affects our choices. If the profit is greater because of the conflict's manifestation and protraction rather than its expiration, the engaged party ensures its manifestation and protraction until the profit is maximized, and avoids putting an end to it (the process may also work in reverse).

Thus, according to case study 6.1, Nick could have profited even through a legal confrontation (e.g. by being indemnified for the unjustified assault and insult suffered at the hands of the unknown driver). The evidence shows that he could also claim compensation for the lost profit from Jim's company.

Negative and positive influences

Negative and positive influences can be difficult to assess, and can only be indirectly calculated in terms of monetary units, as mentioned previously.

Example 6.6   Negative and positive influences

A company is facing intense conflicts with the union leadership and refuses to negotiate despite the obvious financial deficit it suffers. The company decides to adopt this behavior because they intend to subvert the syndicate's union leadership through a new leadership during the upcoming elections. They hope to nominate a new leadership capable of establishing peaceful relationships that will rely on trust and will adapt to the cultural profile of the business.

According to case study 6.1, Nick will probably face some negative repercussions in the event that he engages in a conflict with the unknown driver. Not only will his relationship with Jim be exposed to serious risk of collapsing, but also it would be extremely difficult to preserve his current bonds with his working group should they hold him responsible for losing the project and for all the stress they will have endure to make up for their shortfall. Second, he will run significant professional risks while trying to create a new team capable of offering competitive services.

The only opportunity for Nick to experience positive influences would be to dispense with the work group members that questioned his leadership role. That would give him the chance to create a new team and become involved with an alternative, more profitable and challenging branch of services.

The series of observations lead to the conclusion that a conflict's expiry is achieved whenever its existence brings more negative consequences than positive ones. Conversely, when the positive parameters outnumber the negative ones, the conflict is manifested and protracted proportionally. Regardless of which of the two scenarios occurs, the parties develop strategies for the improvement of their results in order to limit the negative and increase the positive influences.

So, if Nick, despite his preferences, does not manage to avoid conflict with the stranger, he will certainly do his best to reduce the negative influences, increase and utilize the positive ones, and exploit them to develop adequate policies.

Duration of influences

What can easily be observed in conflicts is a plethora of controversial behaviors, such as when we rush to deal with petty conflicts while

> **Example 6.7   Duration of influences**
>
> Mary runs the administrative department of a pharmaceutical company. Every year from December to February – when the time comes to award the annual sales bonus – the same conflict arises between her and her subordinates. The cause of the conflict is that, unlike salespeople, Mary's subordinates do not receive the bonus given at that time. This situation creates a series of tensions and discussions aimed at claiming a raise that would diminish the discrepancy between their salary and that of salespeople. Nevertheless, in March the tension simmers down and the department becomes peaceful once more.

ignoring more significant ones, despite the fact that their protraction is not deliberate.

There are, however, many ways to interpret these behaviors: a basic criterion for interpretation is the *duration of influences*, which determines whether and how we are going to handle the conflict. Put simply: "If the duration of negative influences is short, and the duration of positive influences is long, why bother ending a conflict when it is more advantageous to protract it?" Furthermore, conflicts follow an unstable course with several fluctuations over time. Thus, if we manage to keep the consequences of fluctuations within affordable limits – no matter how inconvenient the conflict's resolution is – it could be more profitable to choose to control the conflict and its restricted tolerance.

What could Mary do to settle the tension, apart from keeping it under control until it simmers down, as happens every year? A significant factor in not satisfying the request of her subordinates is that the cost for the increase in salaries is particularly high and would not be approved by Mary's supervisors.

In addition to this, the duration of influences helps define how a conflict will evolve afterwards, or whether it will give birth to post-conflicts as a result of previous conflict settlements (meta-conflicts). Those who engage in a post-conflict might be the those that participated in the initial conflict or others who joined in later on. This is situation in case study 6.2.

The reasons for the tensions in case study 6.2(a) are multiple and can be expressed in the simple questions:

- How will "difficult" tasks be distributed between the team members?
- How quickly will the tasks be finished?

Case study 6.2   Katrina, her subordinates and Helen

(a) Katrina and her subordinates

Katrina is the manager of a software development department and has eight subordinates working for her. The last two months have been quite tense, as the team was assigned a new project that needs to be presented to an important client. The climate of pressure has pushed two subordinates to threaten to quit their jobs.

1. The program, worth US$1.5 million, must be ready in a month.
2. Katrina aims at preventing or reducing any tension during this month to ensure that high-quality work will be delivered on time.
3. In the event of mistakes or delay, the company will have to pay large penalty fees, for which they will hold Katrina responsible.

(b) Katrina, her subordinates and Helen

It is Monday morning and Katrina receives a message from Helen, the human resources manager of the company, about the completion of construction works in the basement of the main building. Katrina has two days to suggest which three of her subordinates should have their own parking space in the basement of that building. The remaining subordinates should continue to park their cars outside.

4. The parking spaces are quite advantageous because they give access to the offices via an elevator.
5. Conversely, those who park outside need quite some time to find a good parking place and have to walk for at least five minutes to get to the main entrance.
6. The most significant thing, though, is that the privilege of having a personal parking space, exactly as the company executives do, adds prestige.

- What will the resulting quality be?
- Who is responsible for the mistakes?
- Who is going to fix them?

The most significant matter of all, however, is that every subordinate is striving to prove to Katrina that he or she is much more productive and useful than the others and therefore deserves the larger part of the bonus. Katrina is well aware of the fact that the tension will disappear in a month's time, following the successful completion of the work. Therefore, once the project is completed, she will not be the least interested in post-conflicts arising, say, from the way in which the bonus was distributed.

These considerations mean that she chooses a tolerance and conflict control policy. Once the project has been presented, she will be free to involve herself with the conflicts that caused her concern during the preceding period.

In the absence of such circumstances, Katrina would have no difficulty in picking three names. However, based on the current situation, she is afraid that whatever choice she makes some people would be displeased and cause conflicts among those who had been allocated the parking spaces and the others members of the department. Furthermore, post-conflicts would soon arise between the two sides on the basis that she had favored particular employees. Such post-conflicts could have serious repercussions on the quality and delivery of the project by the deadline that could probably affect the relationship between Katrina and her client, or the company management itself.

What first seemed to be a reasonable solution to Katrina was to assign a temporary distribution to Helen in order not to be involved with the issue, even though Helen could spread the information and trigger negative comments about her managerial skills (i.e. people could say: "Isn't she capable of assigning three parking lots to three of her subordinates?"). Besides, that could make others think that Helen executed Katrina's orders because in that way Katrina avoided having to take any responsibility over the names chosen.

6.3 Using criteria for the determination of consequences

Each one of the criteria mentioned leads to a specific benefit or deficit value arising from the cost, the profit, the positive and negative influences, and the duration of influences. Regardless of the volume of benefits or deficits, their significance might vary for every individual.

In other words, it is not necessary to give higher priority to a greater benefit rather than a smaller one.

This is why we should not assign priorities without previously determining the volume of the benefit or deficit – after having checked the consequences – of each criterion. A more thorough explanation of the concept will be provided in the following sections.

Example 6.8   Using criteria to determine conditions

The profit from a lawsuit is expected to amount to US$60,000; the court cost is US$20,000. However, there are no funds available with which to support the litigation. As a result, the priority of covering the US$20,000 expense is higher than that of the expected profit, despite the profit being three times the value.

The source of consequences

Before beginning to choose the conflict handling process, we take into account the fact that we usually have more than just one solution. Therefore, defining the consequence of every possible solution makes it easier to choose the best.

But, even if we do not have the opportunity to choose between a plethora of solutions, it is always useful to determine the source of consequences for the solution we do have. This is a secure way of preparing ourselves to face the upcoming consequences, and developing ways to reduce negative and increase positive aspects of the available solution.

However, finding and defining the consequences is usually a difficult process, mainly because:

- The consequences of the conflict may extend to multiple relationship fields, thus causing collateral repercussions (perhaps even outside the strict relationship framework with the other party).
- The consequences are not homogeneous, since they refer to controversial evidence, such as pragmatic or emotional consequences.
- During the conflict, there could be many parties participating directly or indirectly, which could influence the behavior of the parties involved.

These difficulties are dealt with by using a consequence definition system. According to the system we propose, we seek out the consequences at each stage of the applied model, as presented in Figure 6.2.

Let us take a look at the places where the alternative ways of handling a conflict are sought:

- *On the power reserves* (16): at this stage we examine the increase, decrease, invalidation and upgrading of our powers, as well as those of the other party. The consequences here affect every single stage of the

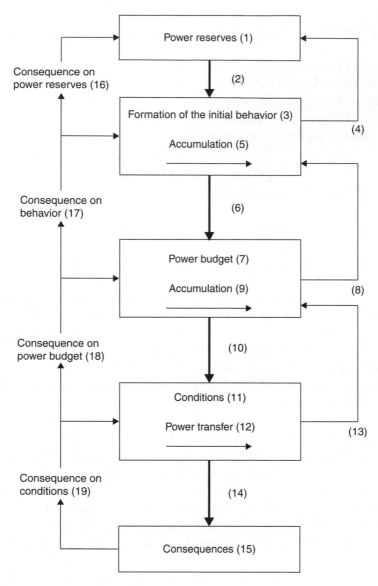

Figure 6.2 Seeking the sources of the consequences

model because the shifts on the power reserves cause the conflict ability and the efficient power use to change (Example 6.9).

- *On the formation of the initial behavior* (17): the consequences of this stage are evident when our actions influence the data included in the conflict behavior of those who participate in the conflict engagement.

Example 6.9   Sources of consequences: power reserves

One may decide to manipulate the other party in order to gain more profit but, ultimately, when the other party becomes aware of this behavior, their prestige and reliability decrease, causing issues in future collaboration with that party or others. In other words, the drop in level of reliability and prestige triggers a reduction of power reserves.

Example 6.10   Sources of consequences: formation of initial behavior

As soon as the other party realizes that they have been manipulated, they decide to take action promptly in order to balance the deficits they have suffered, which is not desired by the manipulative party.

They influence the structure of relationships, the cost of conflict and conflict ability itself (Example 6.10).

- *On the power budget* (18): here, the consequences increase or reduce the engagement fields, both ours and those of adversaries. In the first case, powers are scattered to more fields; in the second, they are significantly restrained. Therefore, when power reserve surplus is constrained, scattering the powers to multiple fields may reduce conflict ability, and vice versa. Within this framework, a shift in the significance level of the fields might also occur; given that the parties invest more power in upgrading fields, and vice versa. To pursue the same example, the applied manipulation strategy makes the other party take steps to counterbalance the shortfall, which ultimately upgrades the significance level of the related field of relationships with the other party. For this reason, the particular conflict field with the party who feels they have been manipulated would need additional power reserves and could cause our power budget to change. The question arises: Are we able to afford an additional burden when we redistribute our restricted power reserves?
- *On conditions* (19): at this particular stage, consequences influence efficiency positively or negatively. Therefore, in order to ascertain the direction of influence, we examine individually the consequences for each type of condition (financial, political, temporal, cultural, legal, technical, complementary), or even the mix of consequences in the particular conflict (Example 6.11).

Example 6.11   Sources of consequences: conditions

The manipulation tactic will make our political conditions harder because it will strengthen the other party when they receive the sympathy of third parties. There will also be problems with legal conditions, in the event of legal charges, or even in terms of cultural conditions, as future transactions could sail under the flag of mistrust and unethical tactics.

Sources and criteria for defining consequences

At this point, based on what has been presented in the preceding section, what we search for when making a choice is:

(a) *The cost and damages*:
  • In the power reserves.
  • In the formation of the initial behavior.
  • In the power budget.
  • In the conditions.

The question awaiting a response is: If we finally make the definite choice, what will be the cost and damages in each of these four stages?

(b) *The profit*:
  • In the power storage.
  • In the formation of the initial behavior.
  • In the power budget.
  • In the conditions.

Here, the query is similar: If we finally make a definite choice, what will be the profit in each of these four stages?

(c) *The positive and negative influences*:
  • In the power storage.
  • In the formation of the initial behavior.
  • In the power budget.
  • In the conditions.

So: If we finally make a definite choice, what will be the positive and negative influences in each of these four stages?

(d) The duration of influences:
- In the power storage.
- In the formation of the initial behavior.
- In the power budget.
- In the conditions.

And once more, if we finally make a definite choice, what will be the duration of positive or negative influences in each of these four stages?

Let us take a look at the ways of defining and evaluating consequences, as presented in case study 6.3.

Case study 6.3   Kevin manipulates the department and the management

(a) Kevin, Stella, Vickie and Jason

Kevin is the managing director of a high-tech medical equipment company that, over the last 18 years, has become a leader in the local market, having a 40 percent share. Stella works as the financial manager and Vickie is her subordinate.

1. Vickie is the supervisor of both the accounting department and the supply chain.
2. Kevin would like to have more power to control the company.
3. To achieve this, he decided to withdraw power from Stella and support Jason, the sales and technical services manager.
4. To achieve his objectives, Kevin aims at assigning the management of the supply chain to Jason.

(b) Kevin, the supply chain, the management board and the consultant

Kevin decides to apply a policy that creates tensions in the supply chain, indicating Stella as being the person mainly responsible for these tensions. The growing tensions soon start worrying the management board, which eventually agrees to Kevin's suggestion to call in an external consultant for an evaluation.

5. Following Kevin's orders, the consultant suggests to assign management of the supply chain to Jason.
6. Because of the multiple tensions, the existing flaws in the supply chain – which Kevin continues to exaggerate – begin to surface.

7. At this point, he requests the dismissal of a very competent supply chain executive –his perfect scapegoat; Stella opposes the request.

(c) Stella, Vickie, Eddie and the supply chain staff

Vickie helps Eddie to resolve practical matters concerning his new position; at the same time, she supports her former subordinates. Six months later, Vickie and Stella agree to stop helping Eddie out. This sudden change leads to large issues related not only to the company's internal operation, but also affects relationships with customers as well.

8. While all this is going on, Vickie has been receiving complaints from her former subordinates about the behavior of Jason and Eddie.
9. Their behavior is in conflict with their cultural details that had been determined when Vickie was their supervisor.
10. Vickie therefore decides to take control of the whole situation by making the staff hope that she will eventually be re-assigned to manage the supply chain department.
11. The way Jason and Eddie behave forces two important executives to resign.

Kevin is confident that he is going to change things within the company, despite the strong resistance Stella and Vickie will put up to his self-seeking purposes. Although the company has no real need to re-assign responsibilities to the staff, he is trying to use devious means to avoid any "collateral damage".

This situation went on for six months, until Kevin had sufficient reasons to suggest that management assign control of the supply chain to Jason. Against all odds, Stella and Vickie finally approve the suggestion.

After this rearrangement, Vickie kept her position as supervisor of the accounting department and she was still Stella's subordinate. Conversely, the entire supply chain staff were moved to the sales department with a new supervisor, Eddie. Stella, and mainly Vickie, offered to train Eddie for his newly assigned duties.

One year later, after having gone through all these problems, the company decides to move control of the supply chain back to the financial services department and nominate Vickie to be the supervisor.

The main reason why Kevin's attempt to change things within the company failed is that he ignored, or did not correctly estimate, the consequences of his choice when he engaged in a conflict with Stella and Vickie in the first place. Apparently, he overestimated his conflict ability and underestimated, or completely ignored, the effectiveness of Stella and Vickie's indirect reactions while making his plans. As a result, when his consequences expanded to a point that jeopardized his other fields, he called off any pre-existing intention.

However, it is not useful to interpret this explanation as a resignation from the scheduled plans in case of unfavorable consequences. Had Kevin foreseen at least some of the consequences, he would have been able to prepare himself adequately (i.e. he could have avoided letting Eddie or the entire supply chain depend on Vickie for so long, and would have probably developed a "plan B" in the event of failure).

Based on case study 6.3, Kevin's consequence definition process is structured as follows:

(a) *The cost and damages*: the cost and damages are caused by:
   - The salary of the new supply chain supervisor.
   - The training cost.
   - The drop in productivity level when passing to a new management.
   - The issues with clients.

   Such matters, however, are expected to arise, as it often happens through organizational changes. Here, the realization and expiry costs were low, whereas the protraction cost kept expanding without determining its final volume, given Stella and Vickie had no reason whatsoever to cease their indirect reactions.

(b) *The profit:* the expected (financial) profit that Kevin would obtain from the conflict was undefined, yet high in the event that he managed to extend his control over the company. Nevertheless, during the course of the conflict the profit was reduced to zero.

(c) *The negative and positive influences:* Kevin's consequences are exclusively negative and have multiple sources. First, the new supervisor depends on Vickie's know-how, and she has no interest in the change whatsoever. In addition to this, she tries to limit the role of the staff in achieving the change by ignoring their cultural and political conditions
   - The cultural ones, due to the different way Vickie managed the department in comparison with Eddie's way.
   - The political ones, due to the relationship of the employees with Vickie and the degree of influence she exercises over them.

   Limiting the significance of these parameters causes the department to malfunction and lose some of the staff (their power reserves decrease), or even credibility to the board of the management. The reason behind this is that the change ultimately proved to be unnecessary and disadvantageous. Consequently, Kevin's future suggestions will be handled with greater caution, and may perhaps lack the full support of the management (negative influence on his political conditions). As the change follows its course, Kevin is burdened with additional conflict tensions, meaning his conflict ability decreases in some fields (e.g. the constantly upgrading "supply chain" field) and he begins to need more powers that he will need to withdraw from his other fields.

(d) *The duration of influences:* each influence within the entire duration of the change has an evident expiry date. What is expected to occur is that:
- The cost will keep growing.
- Kevin's reliability will significantly decrease.
- The tensions and fields of relationships are going to require a larger amount of power from him.
- Kevin's political conditions (third-party support) will only deteriorate.

It is possible that the duration of similar influences will cause trouble that will keep him from engaging in more profitable activities (i.e. planning and realizing strategic alliances to promote the company's products in further markets).

The nature and volume of these consequences suggest that Kevin should have given higher priority to the duration of the constantly growing negative consequences.

On the other hand, Stella and Vickie chose a more intelligent strategy: to apply a concession strategy to Kevin's requests, given they were unable to deal with his devious behavior, either in a direct or indirect way. During the event, however, they cleverly assigned him excessive responsibilities; these caused trouble for the company and forced Kevin to return matters to their previous state.

Put simply, Kevin started the conflict to achieve a win–lose outcome that, against all the odds, resulted in a lose–win outcome. Stella and Vickie's profit not only consisted in avoiding the unprofitable change, but they also ensured that similar incidents with regard to the supply chain department will not take place for some considerable time in the future, regardless of who may try to interfere.

To conclude, each consequence in the analysis could have been predicted by following the suggested process. In addition, we conclude that the determining consequences not only occur during the initial estimations, but also in the course of the conflict when new data emerge (i.e. how the other parties' behavior evolves).

Sources and priorities of criteria

What is crucial when making the final decision, apart from the volume of consequences, is also its significance. This creates a need to define priorities in criteria. Priorities influence the outcome of our choices; for example, we are led to different final choices if we give higher priority to the cost rather than to positive influences.

The priority of a criterion depends on the volume of repercussions and their relative significance. A priority is proportionally higher:

• The larger and heavier the cost or the damage.
• The larger and more indispensable the profit.
• The greater and more unbearable the negative influences.
• The greater and more necessary the positive influences.
• The longer and more unbearable the duration of the negative influences.
• The longer and more indispensable the positive influences.

Overall, if we wish to attribute a quantitative value to priorities, we distribute 10 or 100 units to them according to their significance. In other words, the larger and more significant the consequences caused by a criterion, the more its corresponding units.

The other party's behavior

Based on this way of thinking, we can predict the other party's consequences and priorities and, thus, their behaviors. Even when this behavior diverges from what is universally accepted as "normal behavior", such a divergence can be predicted based on how the other party expands a particular type of consequences. For example, they might be more interested in short-term rather than future profits, even if the future profits are significantly larger. It is, however, generally suggested the more difficult procedure be used to estimate the other party's priorities in order to achieve a more reliable prediction (see Helen's real scenarios in case study 3.2).

6.4 Summary

No matter how efficient a way of handling conflict is, it does not always ensure the desired effects, which is why it is better to seek out the consequences. The search for consequences has relied on criteria such as the cost, the profits, the positive and negative influences, and their duration.

At this point, it is worth stressing that mentioning the criteria without providing guidelines for determining their exact content is an incomplete process. Therefore, we seek their content in every stage of the model: more specifically, the power reserves, the formation of the initial behavior, the way the power reserves (i.e. the power budget) are distributed and the conditions.

Once more, these definitions are not sufficient, since the other party's behavior plays a significant role in the evolution and outcome of negotiations. This is why it has been necessary to include *predictable* behaviors in the content of criteria (i.e. the reactions of the other party). This has been possible due to the explanatory nature of the model under discussion. Therefore, we may be able to predict the other party's behaviors when they are as concerned as we are about the repercussions:

- On their power reserves.
- On the formation of their initial behavior.
- On their power budget.
- On their conditions.

The predictions would be reliable if the other party evaluated their data in a homogeneous way; in other words, if the other party wished and could define the sources of their consequences, and gave to criteria the priority that corresponded to the benefits and deficits we have ascertained. However, since this does not always happen, we offer two possible solutions:

- Discover how the other party evaluates its consequences (e.g. throughout past behaviors). The fact that the other side becomes predictable and that these behaviors diverge from what is considered to be a "normal behavior" not only causes no trouble whatsoever in applying the suggested procedure, but also facilitates the entire process because we feel less uncertain about our choices.
- Shape the other party's behavior in a desirable way. (This alternative will be explored thoroughly in Chapter 7.)

Overall, we are led to the conclusion that:

> The more profitable or less prohibitive the consequences of a conflict, the more we aim at engaging in it, and vice versa.

CHAPTER 7

Ways to handle a conflict

Traditional negotiation strategies, concerning types of direct negotiations, are further broadened to types of virtual negotiations and isolated actions. In complex negotiations, the parties tend to develop mixes of negotiating strategies to improve their effectiveness. In addition, the parties often use incongruent strategies. This chapter stresses the interpretative nature of the proposed concept, which enables both the development and evaluation of such advanced dealings, and the decoding of the other party's negotiating behavior.

So far, we have examined how consequence functions define processes when choosing a particular way to deal with a conflict. In this chapter, with the help of Figure 7.1, we are going to cover these ways in greater detail. Years of research and discussion have proven there are three main ways to handle a conflict:

- Direct negotiations.
- Virtual negotiations.
- Isolated actions.

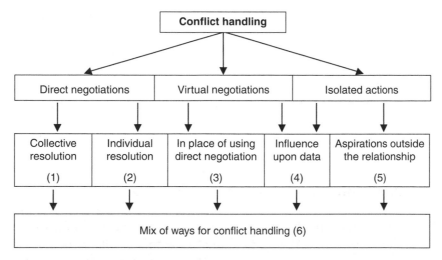

Figure 7.1 Ways to handle a conflict

Example 7.1   Direct and indirect negotiation

An employee that is not satisfied with the level of pay made to him by an employer starts negotiating with the employer about a raise (direct negotiation). Prior to the negotiations, the employee spreads a rumor among his colleagues that he has received valid and better compensated job offers from other companies. The goal here is to perform a virtual negotiation in order to force the employer to make an improved offer. At the same time, the employee applies for other part-time or full-time jobs in a more interesting field (isolated actions). So, if the employee is not granted the raise, he will be able to increase his income by working at a second job.

Direct negotiations occur when the parties are in direct contact in order to work out a solution to their problem. There are two are ways to resolve an issue within *direct communication*: collective communication (1), and individual communication (2).

Indirect or *virtual negotiations* take place either instead of direct negotiation (3), or to influence the other party's conflict data in order to change its negotiating behavior (4).

In isolated actions (5) there are no direct or indirect communications, since the parties behave regardless of their future relationship.

Any of these ways can be used either as a stand-alone solution or in combination with other methods, thus leading to a mix of conflict handling techniques (6) aimed at improving the final result. Put simply, while the various parties negotiate directly, each party attempts individually to influence the others indirectly (i.e. via third parties) and searches for solutions outside the actual negotiating relationship.

These dealings will satisfy both sides (win–win resolution), or just one (win–lose resolution), or no one (lose–lose resolution). So, before proceeding with the analysis of conflict handling ways, it is advisable to define the concepts "win" and "lose."

7.1 "Win" and "lose" concepts in negotiations

Techniques of conflict handling are used with the intention of achieving the desired result. In the event that we achieve this result, we believe that we have "won"; if we do not achieve the desired result, we feel that we have "lost" (Example 7.2).

Example 7.2   "Win" and "lose" concepts in negotiations

(a) The level of demand

If someone wants to sell a piece of real estate at US$354,000 and manages to do so, they will consider they have won. If they fail to find a buyer at that price and finally sell at US$326,000, they will think that they lost.

  If the price of US$326,000 was thought to be satisfactory from the beginning of the transaction, then selling at that amount would cause the owner to believe they had won the negotiation.

(b) Best alternative to a negotiated agreement (BATNA)

If the owner wants to sell at US$354,000 but finally sells at US$326,000, the owner's BATNA is US$310,000, since this price is the best offer received from another interested buyer.

  The terms "win" and "lose" are subjective, as they depend on the level of expectations each of us sets: the higher the expectations, the more likely the outcome will be a "loss".

  An extra criterion for defining when we "win" a negotiation is the widely-used "best alternative to a negotiated agreement" (BATNA). This is the best solution that can be obtained in the event that we do not reach agreement with the other party.

  In example 7.2(b), the fact that the owner managed to achieve US$16,000 of surplus compared with his BATNA (US$310,000) leads us to conclude that the greater the difference is between our BATNA and our finally achieved outcome, the stronger the belief concerning our "win".

  To summarize, winning or losing a negotiation depends mainly on:

- The level of the expectations.
- The extent to which the final outcome meets initial expectations, or minimizes the cost of the conflict leading to the engagement and, thus, to the initial negotiations.
- The difference of value between the BATNA and the outcome actually achieved.

  There are two main reasons why we are interested in the classification of the negotiating outcomes. The first relates to the improvement of the negotiating abilities aimed at compensating for negotiating flaws that leave us short on results compared with others holding the same data.

The second reason is so that we understand what "losing" means to the other party. If they consider they have lost, they will probably, at least, want to counterbalance their loss in the future, which could trigger post-conflicts.

Thus, the larger the other party's loss, the more eager they would be to counterbalance that loss. Reaching these conclusions helps us develop policies to:

- Avoid a large cost of post-conflicts.
- Set limits to the other party's losses.
- Counterbalance the other party's loss in a variety of ways.

The core of these policies is to protect ourselves from the other party's desire for revenge in our future negotiations.

7.2 Direct negotiations

Despite any clarification made so far, one question remains to be answered: To what extent may some forms of "face-to-face" encounter or communication be considered as direct negotiations? The mere fact that two parties meet, sometimes as a pretext to gain time or to damage the other party, does not constitute a direct negotiation. Rather, for "face-to-face" encounters or communication to be considered as direct negotiations there should be the intention of *resolving the matter*, even with the direct participation of authorized third parties (i.e. consultants, representatives, mediators and so on).

Direct negotiation, which includes the *resolution* of either a *collective* or *individual* conflict, occurs when:

- The parties choose it as the best way to resolve the problem.
- The parties are forced to use it because their data do not allow the application of any other method.

Collective resolution

Collective settlement constitutes the foundation stone of the Program on Negotiation at Harvard University. According to the Program, the most

---

Example 7.3   Interest-based bargaining

A wants to sell a business for US$778,000, and B wants to buy it for US$707,000. In this case, the primary aspirations are to earn US$778,000 and to pay US$707,000.

---

effective way of negotiating is the *interest-based bargaining* of the parties (rather than *positional bargaining*). Interest-based bargaining is built upon a collective effort to resolve the conflict within a relationship.

The main reason why interest-based bargaining is preferred over positional bargaining is because the parties' positions are usually incompatible with each other (Example 7.3).

When negotiation are based on the parties' positions, win–lose or lose–lose outcomes are often the result. Lose–lose outcomes occur when both sides experience shortfalls – either because they could not reach agreement, or because the outcome was unprofitable for both of them (i.e. in Example 7.3, a US$736,000 outcome). So, according to the Program on Negotiation, the bargaining leads to either a dead-end or a faulty result for at least one of the parties.

Figure 7.2 overleaf presents the process of interest-based bargaining during which X and Y have determined their positions (3 and 4) before engaging in the negotiation. However, each of these positions is the product of their interests. In other words, X's position is based on their own interests X1, X2, X3 (1), as follows for Y with Y1, Y2, Y3 (2).

In order to avoid bargaining their positions (3 and 4) and ending up in an interest-based bargaining situation, X and Y need to establish their interests (5 and 6) without projecting their positions.

Once this process is completed, each party points out their own interests (5 and 6) and, in this way, they are collectively looking for solutions that combine and cover both parties' interests (7). So, when the interests of both parties are fulfilled, their initial positions are indirectly respected; thus, the conflict is resolved. The parties jointly find a solution to a problem that includes their interests. Their outcome is one of mutual gain (i.e. a win–win resolution).

The only way to achieve a solution like this is to have compatible interests, which usually are "hiding" behind apparently incompatible positions. It is important to stress that the combination of interests is based on the concept that what is significant for one party might not be so for the other: X aims to cover interests that are important to Y but trivial to X, and vice versa.

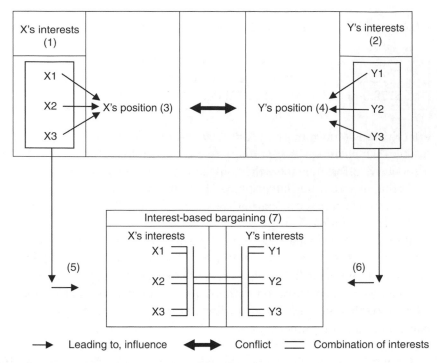

Figure 7.2   Interest-based and positional bargaining

Example 7.4   Collective resolution

X claims the benefit of 50 units and Y claims the benefit of 70 units. To cover their requirements, the total benefit should be 120 units; but only 100 units are available. However, if X and Y engage in interest-based bargaining, the total benefit could grow to 120 and they could achieve what, at first glance, seemed impossible.

The partnership between the various parties for the fulfillment of mutual gain leads to 2 + 2 = 5 synergies, where the final value is greater than that expected.

Hence, the main ambition of this concept is to create the initial existing value. Researchers of this concept believe that it is the most favorable option to be applied when:

• The parties have to cope with multiple issues, meaning combinations can be created of their "most significant" and "least significant" issues.

- There are going to be long-term relationships that will keep one party from causing losses for the other. Causing losses could make the other party want to get even in a future negotiation, which could counterbalance previous concessions towards the other party.
- Each party aims as much at their individual gain as at a mutual gain, as a precondition of their individual profit.

The next two case studies describe the method that is used to settle problems collectively within a negotiation. Case study 7.1 presents a more stereotypical form of the model, while case study 7.2 shows divergence and some possible consequences of its application.

The mediator discovered that Pit and Elinor had engaged in positional bargaining. Either the negotiation was a perfect dead-end and led to a win–lose resolution, or, if they finally agreed to the happy medium of a 20-minute break for every one hour and 30 minutes worked, they would be led to a lose–lose resolution.

The mediator therefore decided to change their negotiating method, and applied interest-based bargaining. He asked them to give the reasons upon which they built their positions:

- Pit wanted to keep the labor cost low. If the union achieved its goals, the labor cost would increase by 17 percent, which would worsen the financial situation of the business.

Case study 7.1   Casino "Kings": Pit, Elinor and the mediator

Pit, (the spokesman for Casino Kings) and Elinor (the representative of the casino's union) intend to sign a collective agreement relating to the salaries' and improved working conditions for the casino's employees.

1. The biggest problem that needs to be settled is the break time on the production floor (the roulette and blackjack tables).
2. Until today, Pit had allowed staff on the roulette and blackjack tables a 20-minute break for every one hour and 40 minutes worked.
3. Elinor demands a 20-minute break for every one hour and 20 minutes worked, which would reduce the daily working time of the affected employees.
4. Given that, so far, the two sides had failed to settle the issue, they called on a mediator for help.

- Elinor demanded the fulfillment of the recommendations set by the national branch union of casino employees, which had managed to establish the working conditions Elinor repeatedly requested in all the casinos across the country. What she feared most was that keeping things the way they were at "Kings" could cause other casinos to resume the same regime.

In the course of discussions, it came about that the working schedule of the business fluctuated. Every weekday and weekend from July to August, as well as during the 15 days of the Christmas and New Year's Eve holidays, "Kings" had an enormous workload. The same tight schedule continued almost all year, particularly on Thursdays, Fridays and Saturdays. The other days of the week, during the remaining months of the year, the workload was significantly reduced.

These details, together with the fact that the parties avoided tension – due to the mediator's intervention – successfully resolved the issue, resulted in the following agreement being reached:

(a) The work schedule would remain unchanged in July and August, during the 15 days of the Christmas and New Year's Eve holidays, and from Thursday to Saturday all the year, (a 20-minute break for every one hour and 40 minutes worked).
(b) On the remaining days of the year, the employees are to take a 20-minute break for every one hour worked.

Overall, the outcome of the negotiation was considered to be a win–win resolution: both sides came out on top. The business avoided the 17 percent rise in labor costs; the workers opened a new channel for the future improvement of working conditions on the production floor. This procedure represents a classical application of interest-based bargaining, because it finally led to a common profit and covered all the interests of the parties.

Conversely, in case study 7.2 it has not been possible to obtain a common profit, which is why it has been sought at the expense of third parties.

Due to the circumstances, Al thought that the preconditions of the situation were compatible with interest-based bargaining: hence, he chose the win–win concept. First, he explained the core of the people's interests, both to the Mayor and to Harry; then, he looked for the other two parties' interests and worked out a way to satisfy them. Al's behavior reassured the Mayor regarding her suspicion of the opposition's involvement in the neighborhood's request to move the market elsewhere. As a result, the three parties moved on to find a collective solution: thus, the participants of the conflict became "problem solvers". Each party's interests are listed in Table 7.1 in the way in which they were presented during their negotiations.

Case study 7.2   Al, the Mayor and Harry

Al is the town hall representative of the residents of an area that, over the last few years, has started to become overpopulated. He therefore decided to take action in order to move the street market away from the neighborhood. For 30 years, the street market has been open every Monday for six months of the year, despite the fact that legislation only allows it to be open for four months. For some considerable time, the newly-elected Mayor has refused to discuss residents' concerns, believing them to have been stirred up by the opposition (for many years, there had been no complaints about the market). Furthermore, she firmly believes that, by delaying dealing with the matter, the residents' agitation would eventually simmer down.

1. What she hoped to achieve did not come about; the conflict grew larger.
2. Harry, who represented the street market vendors, supported the Mayor.
3. Apart from the three main participants (Al, the Mayor and Harry) there were also secondary parties:
   - The town hall's opposition.
   - The street market customers.
   - The citizens.
   - The local mass media.

Against all odds, the collective effort to settle the conflict did lead to a solution: move the street market to a wider, larger and less-populated street. The new location was expected to allow a more comfortable arrangement of the vendors' stalls; at the same time, municipal funds would increase due to the larger number of vending licenses that could be issued. Nevertheless, since no one knew whether the larger street would ensure the vendors a profit, it was decided that the transfer would be only temporary until they received clear feedback regarding the situation. To lessen the possible reaction of the residents of the new neighborhood, the Mayor excused them from payment of water rates for two reasons:

(a) The city was supplied by its own aqueduct.
(b) The few people living in the new market location would only result in a small shortfall to municipal funds.

Table 7.1   The interests of the parties regarding the street market

The parties	The interests
The neighborhood residents	• Eradicate the street market-related crime: petty thefts, burglaries, car thefts and general damages. • Avoid the burden of moving their cars to another street the day before. • Keep the neighborhood as clean as it is before the street market opens (the street cleaners are usually unable to restore the area fully at the end of the day; there is also a great deal of noise and the shouting of vendors at the crack of dawn is really unbearable). • When the market is open, utility vehicles, such as ambulances, cannot approach the neighborhood. • Potential buyers hold back from renting or buying real estate in the premises, thus lowering real estate values.
The mayor	• Fulfill the basic needs of the majority of citizens, who shop at the street market. • Avoid letting her political status be affected by this conflict or the opposition. • Preserve the municipal funds, which keep growing thanks to the street market taxes.
Harry	• Preserve the vendors' income. • Avoid the stress of moving the market to another location and having to reassign the stands to the vendors.

However, the people living in the new market location were not informed that they would only receive this benefit until such time as the city joined the central water supply unit.

Two months later, since the vendors' profit did not seem to have suffered any damage whatsoever and the affected residents had displayed no objection to the street market, the new location was considered permanent.

If we attempt to look for the possible reasons why the residents of the second location did not react adversely to the decision, we will find that:

(a) They were not fully aware of the inconvenience the street market caused (in the way residents of the first neighborhood had experienced it).

(b) Their conflict intensities were significantly reduced when they excused from paying water rates. The significance of this particular factor leads us to assume they are in receipt of low incomes.

(c) They believed they had low conflict ability, because of their small number and their political inability to cause any shortfall to the Mayor.

Regardless of these parameters, though, the successful outcome of the conflict would not have resulted unless there was the opportunity to move the cost of the conflict resolution to a third party (the residents of the new location).

Individual resolution

During a negotiation concerning individual conflict resolution, it could be that the parties consider the total benefit insufficient for all those with a claim (claiming value approach), which means that, in order to "win", they have to make others "lose". This is the case when all parties engage in positional bargaining in order to limit the aspirations of their adversaries and to maximize their own gain.

Undoubtedly, it is the more powerful party that has the better chances of winning in individual resolution, as this party has a better BATNA and depends less on the outcome. Such a negotiation is limited on the upper part of Figure 7.2, on points (3) and (4), where the parties make use of positional bargaining. According to the Program on Negotiation, it would be better to avoid positional bargaining, which would be ineffective for the following reasons:

- Negotiations often lead to failure when none of the parties backs off at the other party's request.
- Such failure leaves its mark on future relationships, either because the previous negotiations were unsuccessful, or because the party who loses is eventually going to try to make up for their deficits.
- The time needed to reach a final outcome is much longer compared with that required in interest-based bargaining (usually, in this situation, one party bears the pressure and requests of the other side for quite some time).

I would like to add to these arguments an observation from my personal experience in the field of negotiation exercises for educational purposes. When preconditions exist for successful interest-based bargaining but the participants prefer to use positional bargaining instead, even if their outcome could be not considered as lose–lose (because this outcome is better than their BATNA), their total profit will be usually smaller compared with the profit achieved through interest-based bargaining.

To simplify the idea, let us take a look at the specific preconditions for positional bargaining, which are the opposite of those required for interest-based bargaining:

- There is only one interest (single issue), which excludes the possibility of creating multiple combinations of the more and less significant interests in order to maximize the common gain.
- Since the different parties cannot or do not wish to have future relationships, they have no remorse about inflicting considerable damage on the other party.

- Each party's primary goal is to have an individual – not mutual – gain in terms of emotional or pragmatic purposes. For example, if both parties obtain some benefits, one party could boost their powers to cause serious future problems.

Case studies 7.3 and 7.4 analyze the practice behind the positional bargaining. Case study 7.3 depicts the more stereotypical form; case study 7.4 presents some variations leading to multiple interpretations.

Peter had been involved in the hospitality industry for one year and his experience to date had given him the impression that the hotel's main income derived from one-off visitors. This meant he could see no advantage in developing relationships with customers. Furthermore, he firmly believed that the rooms of the Blue Star Hotel, priced at US$99, were a real bargain compared with the rooms in three-star hotels, priced at US$77. He therefore offered her a room for US$92. However, accepting this offer would have meant that Vickie exceeded her budget, and also would have had to pay for any meals out of her own pocket.

Case study 7.3   Peter negotiates with Vickie at the Blue Star Hotel

Vickie, a commercial representative in charge of a large geographical area, travels a great deal in the provinces in order to meet clients. The average duration of these trips is three days. The company provides US$110 to cover hotel and other expenses (Vickie pays approximately US$70 for the hotel and US$40 for breakfast and lunch). The majority of meetings take place in X city which she has visited 15 times in the last eight months alone. However, she usually stays at three-star hotels and has, thus, ensured lower prices corresponding to her budget, position and frequent visits.

1. An important reason permitting her to book at reduced prices is that the average annual booking rate of local hotels is 65 percent.
2. During her most recent stay in the city, she tried to book at the four-star Blue Star Hotel for the very first time.
3. In the lounge she met Peter, the reception shift leader.
4. Vickie explained to him the purpose of her trip, and began negotiating over the terms of her stay.

Her first move was to explain her problem to Peter and to try to develop a creating value approach in order to achieve mutual gain, but her action was in vain. She pointed out that, if they agreed to a better price, her company would choose the hotel for future visits, or perhaps even corporate events (she bluffed on this point, knowing he would not be able to confirm that information). At that point, Peter invited Vickie to check the rooms herself in order to make comparison with other hotels in the area. Vickie refused, and felt quite uncomfortable that she had exposed her interests to a stranger, had wasted her time, and had become the weak player in the engagement. To cut a long story short, she left to book into one of the hotels at which she had previously stayed.

Based on the details of this case study, reaching any agreement would have been extremely difficult as Peter paid great attention to short-term profit and refused to consider any positive influence (i.e. corporate events organized by Vickie at the hotel, or their long-term relationship). The most plausible explanation for this behavior was either that the Blue Star Hotel was always fully booked, or that Peter had received clear guidelines from the management.

On the other hand, the criterion that was most significant to Vickie was the cost. Her intention to draw Peter's attention to future profit failed, since Peter's priority on this criterion was low. Overall, the failure of this negotiation was highly probable. Perhaps there would have been a greater chance of achieving a positive outcome if Vickie had asked to speak with the hotel manager in the hope that the manager was able to be more flexible. However, she avoided doing so for several reasons (e.g. Peter had already triggered a strong emotional conflict, and Vickie did not wish to make this worse in the event that she failed to achieve her aims when speaking with his supervisor).

Case study 7.4 presents a variation of standard positional bargaining that eventually results in a peculiar win–win outcome.

Of the three carriers that participated in the competition, two were immediately dismissed for reasons of protocol (that meant that their offers were not going to be considered at all). These two companies objected to the decision, but their objection was over-ruled. The competition was therefore won by Mobile Phone, since their offer was less than the annual budget Vehicular Access had decided to invest in mobile phones for their personnel. The competition announcement set the cooperation period at two years, with the possibility of extending the contract for a further year (this was an exclusive privilege for Vehicular Access).

Despite the fact that Mobile Phone had won the competition, Georgia had to adhere to the internal regulations of Vehicular Access and negotiate

Case study 7.4   A large mobile phones deal: Georgia vs. Anna

Georgia and Anna had to negotiate cooperation between their companies, the "Vehicular Access" transport company and the carrier "Mobile Phone". Vehicular Access is the largest transport company in town, with 3,000 buses and 9,000 employees, and carrying out 15,000 trips each day, servicing 1.4 million people.

1. Vehicular Access announced a competition, with the award to the lowest bidder, to give free mobile phones with free connection contracts to 6,200 employees.
2. The competition concerned the supply of 6,200 mobile devices, SIM cards, batteries, power adapters, wired hands-free sets, and leather sleeves.
3. The competition also included a maximum prepaid talk time included in the connection contract of the 6,200 employees that was also going to be covered by Vehicular Access.
4. Additional talk time would be charged directly to the users.

with Anna for a further price reduction. The internal regulations mentioned negotiation for the further improvement of the price in the event that the competition received only one valid offer.

There were other more personal reasons why Georgia wanted to prove that she protected the company's interests by reducing Anna's price. In addition to this, she had to include in the price the replacement of the wired hands-free kits with wireless ones, which was not mentioned in the first announcement. This replacement was compulsory due to the recently revised Road Traffic Act, which only allowed bus drivers to speak on the phone through wireless hands-free sets.

Anna presented an offer of US$8 including the device, the accessories, and the free talk time. In the meantime, Georgia was seeking a valid reason to support her request for a further discount, and she finally found it:

Put simply, both parties – triggered by quite different motivations – rushed to sign up to the agreement.

(a) Mobile Phone was afraid of losing the competition if, in the event that the negotiating process went on for too long, the committee decided to repeat the competition. Needless to say, if matters evolved in this way,

Table 7.2   Georgia's and Anna's negotiation

Contact 1

Georgia: "Your offer should include wireless hands-free kits, which are the only ones approved by the recently revised Road Traffic Act".
(She attempts to adapt the offer to new data).

Anna: "Since the wireless kits were not mentioned in the initial contest terms, we will have to raise the price by US$0.7 per device to meet the new standards. So, the offer is for US$8.7 per month".
(She tries to exploit the new data).

Contact 2

Georgia: "How much do you charge for each X-type device?"
(She seeks Anna's weak points).

Anna: "We offer an overall price, hence we cannot present a price list for each service"
(She speaks evasively).

Contact 3

Georgia: "In order to proceed with our conversation, I need to have more information about the transaction terms. Of course, in the event that you will not provide me with the required details, the company's management will cancel the contest".
(She threatens Anna and, at the same time, exploits her unfavorable BATNA).

Anna: "We have estimated the device in question for US$100".
(Her bad BATNA forces her to reply).

Contact 4

Georgia: "The price you are suggesting is twice as expensive as any gross supply product of the same line".
(In order to reduce the price, Georgia had previously carried out a market poll to be well-informed).

Anna: "Keep in mind that your company has the exclusive right to renew the contract at its expiration and protract it for a further year. What is more, according to the written agreement, we are bound to replace the existing devices with new ones. Should this happen, how are we going to cover the expense of two devices per user within three years?"
(She struggles to justify the high price of the mobile phones).

Contact 5

Georgia: "Are you, perhaps, trying to charge our company with the device replacement cost in case of a future contract renewal? Did you consider that, in two years' time, the devices will be obsolete and worth half their price?"
(She keeps pushing Anna on the points on which she is most vulnerable).

Anna: "Still, who is going to cover the replacement cost?"
(She tries to escape from Georgia's pressure).

Contact 6

Georgia: "Unfortunately, I cannot make the management board accept your proposal; the devices are very expensive at the moment, and are expected to lose 50 percent of their value within two years. Thus, we request a 25 percent discount on the US$8 monthly per user rate of the phone, including a wireless hands-free set".
(She shifts the responsibility to the management board to avoid engaging in a personal conflict with Anna. However, the level of the claimed discount was, by chance, determined by Georgia).

(*continued*)

Table 7.2   Continued

Anna:	"I am sorry but I cannot agree to the discount you are suggesting, since I have no authorization to grant more than 10 percent reduction". (She aims at limiting Georgia's claim for 25 percent discount to 10 percent).
Contact 7	
Georgia:	"If this is the case, the contest is going to be canceled". (She proceeds basing her negotiating strategy on Anna's unfavorable BATNA).
Anna:	"I am going to bring your point to the managing director's attention". (She does not want Georgia to think that she has the authorization to grant a larger discount). (Once this conversation was over, Anna came back offering a 15 percent discount. In addition to this, Mobile Phone intends to return to Vehicular Access the amount of profit they will obtain if they do not replace the phones after two years). (To avoid greater pressure, she grants this non-replacement indemnity knowing that very few users would ever keep their old mobile phone).
Contact 8	
Georgia:	"Still, the 15 percent discount is not sufficient. If you cannot make a better offer, we are going to announce a new contest. Of course, if you grant us the desired reduction in price, our company is more than willing to advertise your operator inside and outside our buses. (She keeps aiming at a better offer, only that this time she also presents a huge advantage for the other side. Georgia is well aware of the fact that she will be evaluated according to the results she achieves on the company's behalf).
Anna:	"I will inform the managing director about your requests as soon as possible". (She refers back to her supervisor, because she does not want to be held responsible for failing in the bargaining).

Final outcome

The managing director of Mobile Phone spoke with his peer at the Vehicular Access and offered 20 percent discount, on condition that they would promptly sign the agreement. Moreover, Vehicular Access will refund within two years the amount corresponding to the non-replaced devices, and is bound to advertise the operator inside and outside their buses.

the company and all of its executives would suffer considerable damages to their interests.

(b) The contract between Vehicular Access and its previous service operator was going to expire in two weeks' time. The company dreaded the possibility of having to pay the staff's mobile phone bills in cash for three months (i.e. until a new contest was held to nominate a new mobile phone partner, since they would not be able to provide the devices).

Case study 7.4 displays the individual resolution tactic, in which the interests of the other party are only slightly taken into consideration and the parties do not collectively resolve the problem. This specific negotiation was based upon Georgia's threatening to repeat the contest, given that she was well aware of Anna's bad BATNA.

On the other hand, Anna herself chose not to respond to Georgia's unfavorable BATNA, although she knew that in the event that the contest was repeated, the staff would strongly react to delaying the provision of free mobile devices. Luckily, this proved to be a smart move, because she avoided bringing additional and dead-end intensities into the negotiation.

Another important consideration is closely connected to who ultimately obtained the greater total benefit because, despite the fact that Georgia succeeded in receiving a 20 percent discount, she did not estimate how much Vehicular Access would make out of selling the advertisements on its 15,000 buses – 1.4 million passengers every day – either to another mobile phone operator or to some other company. In three years, the profit could exceed 50 percent of the annual amount Vehicular Access needs to pay to Mobile Phone.

Against all odds, Anna seems to have received greater benefits, although she had been pushed by Georgia to yield.

Effective direct negotiation

At this point, it would not be incorrect to jump to the conclusion that the collective resolution of an issue constitutes the most useful direct

---

Example 7.5   Effective direct negotiation

In a negotiation between A and B, following which there will be no future involvement, A believes it is more appropriate to proceed with individual resolution and a win–lose outcome, which is what eventually takes place. In the meantime, however, player B conveys the negative feedback of their relationship with A to third parties that will be developing transactions with A in the future. What B achieves is to make the third parties adopt an equally negative behavior towards A, proportional to that which B would display if obliged to negotiate with A for newly-emerged issues. The conclusion from this is that A should have been better off to undertake interest-based bargaining and ensure future relationships, even though his direct relationship with B is only short-term.

negotiation tool: everybody wins, obtains future benefits, and is more productive in further negotiations. However, the Harvard Program on Negotiation points out the preconditions for using this model, which, in my opinion, should be interpreted through extended examination.

From this, we could draw the conclusion that, when the main presuppositions are met, then the parties follow the concept of interest-based bargaining. However, relevant research proves quite the opposite: parties follow the win–lose concept that often becomes a lose–lose result for four main reasons:

- *Lack of the necessary know-how to achieve a collective resolution*: to settle any matter collectively, one must know specific techniques concerning the way the parties:
  - Present their interests;
  - Convince the other party to follow the same path;
  - Build relationships upon trust;
  - Cooperate to find a win–win outcome, even if there is a negative background in their relationships;
  - Handle their anxiety or panic, as well as that of the other party, because they risk experiencing a loss in the event of failure.

  Should there be lack of know-how, one tackles the problem individually, seeking a solution for achieving his own goals.
- *Inability to combine the various interests*: often, parties fail to combine their interests in such a way as to increase their mutual benefits significantly. If such failure is not due to the objective impossibility of combining interests, then we should blame it on the parties' lack of creativity. In such cases, the participation of a third party can improve this creativity, as happened at the Kings Casino (case study 7.1).
- *The way to evaluate consequences*: the selection of the negotiating strategy also depends on the evaluation of consequences – how much we will win or lose, whether consequences will be positive or negative, and for how long these consequences will last. Each player evaluates these parameters and the BATNA differently, that is why one party eventually chooses interest-based bargaining. Someone else might prefer positional bargaining, because he assumes that he will achieve more profit. Another sign of the various evaluation methods is the fact that participants often shift their behavior in the course of negotiations. For example, they can begin with positional bargaining, then proceed with to interest-based bargaining and, after a while, shift again to a different type of negotiating process.

- *The cultural details of the parties*: there are many who believe that mutual profit is just wishful thinking and that a shared benefit does not last long, or even that communicating their interests makes them appear weak in front of the others, or even themselves. According to Harvard's Program on Negotiation, these are the so-called "hard" negotiators, who represent approximately 70 percent to 80 percent of negotiators before being trained in interest-based bargaining. (I had the opportunity to ascertain this during my involvement in training seminars.)

In my opinion, when we have decided to follow the direct negotiation approach, or when we are obliged to negotiate directly, it is more suitable to begin with the interest-based concept, since we are not aware, *a priori*, of the compatibility level between our interests and those of the other side. If we do so – it is of no consequence if we run into negotiating dead-ends – we are always able to change the approach to the other party and apply positional bargaining.

In the event that we adopt the alternative strategy, however, we should be prepared to face serious trouble when finally engaging in an interest-based process. The main reason behind this is that the preceding positional bargaining approach creates tensions which do not allow participants to create an ideal climate for trust that empowers them to settle the issue. This is the situation where a specialized mediator can change the climate and contribute towards a win–win resolution.

Effective collective resolution

In order for a collective resolution to be successful, we make use of two criteria:

- The cost of the total benefits resulting from the collective effort of the parties.
- The additional benefit that was obtained by each side.

The total benefits resulting from the collective efforts of the parties may have different values (e.g. $2 + 2 = 5$ or $2 + 6 = 6$ or $2 + 2 = 7$). The more the parties manage to create the total value, and thus their mutual gain, the more effective is their overall negotiation. However, we should not forget that creating mutual gain is not an end in itself but, rather, the means for growing their individual gain. Thus, one party's effectiveness through collective resolution ultimately concerns each party's ability to achieve additional gain for themselves.

In this way, if one party contributes in expanding the total benefit – say, 2 + 2 = 7 – but only achieves 2, then that party may not be considered effective. This happens mainly when one party feels sufficiently confident about claiming the other party's additional benefit and is intending its acquisition.

To conclude, the parties may initially engage in interest-based bargaining, expand their total benefit, and then proceed with hard positional bargaining to distribute that additional benefit. This may lead them to a win–lose or even a lose–lose outcome, due either to disagreement or the breaking off of negotiations.

Effective individual resolution

Effectiveness at an individual level depends on the value of the benefit one party manages to obtain from all the other players. This is the case of either the claiming value (2 + 2 = 4) or the creating (2 + 2 = 5) value, given that the target is the greater part of the profit, which may also consist of the other party's deficit.

7.3 Virtual negotiations

What is really worth observing when dealing with negotiations is that people often avoid using the standard procedure of direct negotiation and adopt, instead, indirect, virtual negotiation. The two main reasons for this shift of behavior are that direct negotiation:

- Is unattainable, and thus we are obliged to conduct virtual negotiations.
- Is unprofitable and unachievable, meaning that virtual negotiation can better tackle our interests.

Virtual negotiation: why the direct approach is unachievable

Let us say, for example, that X wishes to negotiate with a large number of players (say, 100,000 individuals), and build up relationships, make them buy X's products, convince them to provide support in the event of conflicts between X and any third party, and ease X's tensions. Would it ever be possible for X to negotiate with each player individually to achieve X's goals? The answer is naturally "No". The solution is to develop strategies (public relations, advertising, systems for corporate governance and/or social responsibility and so on), that simultaneously fulfill each objective in terms of these 100,000 players.

Such strategies include arguments, data and information that is also available to any direct negotiation with each individual player. In addition, X is meant to deal with interests and express any intention of fulfilling them successfully (in such a way as to lead to a "win").

Possible reasons for the failure of these strategies are:

- The obtained benefits from the other side are smaller than their bottom line.
- Their winnings are insufficient in terms of the type, value and duration of what is asked in return (i.e. to consume our products or to take action for our support).
- Their "win" is worse than their BATNA; in other words, these people can come up with better solutions in order to obtain greater benefits than those X has offered to them.

These three reasons for turning down an offer may, of course, lead direct negotiations to fail even if they had been undertaken individually with each player.

There are two disadvantages with this type of virtual negotiations in comparison with direct negotiations. It may take so long to conduct the virtual negotiation that there is insufficient time to make any adjustments before the results of the virtual negotiations are required. This limitation is not present in direct negotiations, since the parties can revise their behavior immediately, according to the needs and the ongoing nature of the negotiations.

Second, when virtual negotiations aim simultaneously to affect many persons (e.g. public relations), there are obstacles in combining the different interests of all the parties involved. Conversely, in direct negotiations one has the opportunity to develop a tailor-made means of handling the situation and, thus, to adjust one's behavior to the needs of the other party. This means that, in comparison with direct negotiations, the virtual process lacks *flexibility*.

In conclusion, with virtual negotiations any risk and consequence of failure is experienced to a greater extent. This is why virtual negotiations are only preferred when it is not possible to achieve direct negotiations, as is the situation in case study 7.5:

Case study 7.5   Tina, Alice, and the merger of Chemicals S.A.

Cure S.A, a leader in pharmaceuticals, has recently merged with Chemicals S.A., one of the 12 largest companies in the sector, in order to take advantage of their market and exploit a newly developed, promising drug.

1. To realize the project, they had to keep the Chemical staff from quitting before passing on their knowledge and know-how to Cure executives.
2. Once Cure acquired this know-how, however, a significant number of the Chemical staff could be dismissed, since they would be redundant.
3. Tina took on the task of keeping Chemical personnel within the company until they passed on their know-how. In this, Tina had the help of Alice, a former Chemical employee who had been involved in this merger.
4. Alice's support was indispensable, since the realization of aims was difficult for Tina because of the likelihood that most of Chemical personnel would be taken on by other companies in the sector.

Tina and Alice agreed to use the following policies to ensure the successful realization of the project:

(a) Schedule briefings between the two companies' representatives without giving signals of Cure's intention to replace the Chemical staff.
(b) Reassure Chemical employees that there will be no dismissals.
(c) Allow Chemical employees to retain their position and tasks. However, their subordinates would be Cure employees in order that they could be trained properly to fill the same positions, without Chemical employees becoming aware of this.
(d) Organize social events and trips to strengthen the ties between the personnel of the two companies.

It is important to notice, however, that after a while, although all these measures had been undertaken properly, it became very difficult to keep former Chemical personnel from leaving the company. This development is significantly strengthened by Cure's top management decisions, which

Tina could not change. These decisions triggered tensions within the Chemical personnel and staff:

(a) It was decided to locate both companies in the same building, in order to "facilitate the collaboration among employees and save them time when moving within offices". Nevertheless, they found themselves sharing five to an office, whereas previously they had had their own.
(b) The fact they had no access to Cure's parking area meant they wasted precious time getting to the office building.
(c) They were subject to Cure's bonus system, causing falls in their income.
(d) The leaders of the project decided to do away with any trips offered to them as an extra reward. At that point, in order to minimize any discontent, they were offered holiday bonus packages provided that they met all company targets (unfortunately, this barely made up for the loss of the trips).
(e) The Cure leadership style was less participative than of Chemical; this eventually caused the Chemical staff to suspect that they were only being used to provide information.

Once the general climate of dissatisfaction emerged, Tina and Alice shifted their policy. They proposed a system of voluntary retirement to the Chemical employees, with a large golden handshake and on the condition that they would stay in the company for three further months to train Cure staff. In addition, Chemical executive and staff company cars were replaced with more expensive vehicles of the same quality as those of Cure employees, which they could continue to use for one month following their voluntary retirement.

Despite all these efforts, people ultimately left the company and Cure's financial share proved to be less than had been anticipated before the merger. Three years later, Cure is still operating with a reduced staff and checks the market for new personnel.

Why did they fail to keep Chemical employees within the company until such time as they had passed on their knowledge to Cure specialists? Generally speaking, it could be said that Tina did not correctly estimate the BATNA of Chemical employees. Her offers were insufficient; they merely ensured continued employment – not only at worse terms than previously, but also under worse conditions than their BATNA, considering the working conditions they could have obtained from other companies in the sector.

What had, by that point, become clear to Chemical employees was that Cure could not guarantee their future in the company, since they were obviously only required in order to pass on their know-how. Offering them more expensive cars would never be sufficient to prevent them from quitting.

Overall, Cure could have ensured that the employees with unfavorable BATNAs stayed (i.e. those for whom it would be difficult to find alternative employment). However, Cure was not the least interested in them.

Put simply, according to the criteria we use for the determination of consequences, Cure focused on the *cost*, instead of the *profit*, which also explained why they decided to merge with Chemical.

Virtual negotiation: affecting the negotiating data

The achievement of the desired "win" in a negotiation often meets many obstacles because of the other party's objectives, conditions and so on. Hence, success depends largely on our ability to change these data. Such changes may be in conflict with the other party's interests and thus it is possible they may resist. For this reason, we have to include in the goals of this type of virtual negotiation the way we will anticipate the other party's reactions.

For this purpose, it is advisable to determine the data that need to be changed to eliminate any obstacle. These data – analyzed in previous chapters and included in the various procedural stages – affect the other party's negotiating behavior as much as they affect ours; for example:

- Their power reserves.
- The elements that influence their initial conflict behavior.
- The way they structure their power budget.
- Their conditions.
- Their consequences.

Figure 7.3 shows player A's opportunities to influence player's B negotiating data. Player A's intentions during a negotiation can be multiple, according to the nature of the "wins". We therefore refer to the following indicators:

Powers decay: A aims at reducing B's power reserves in order to decrease their competitiveness, and can achieve this in many ways. For example, cutting B off from the power sources (1), negatively affects both B's conflict ability (2 and 3) and effectiveness (4). Then, by cultivating B's conflict intensities (2) and expanding B's fields of third-party

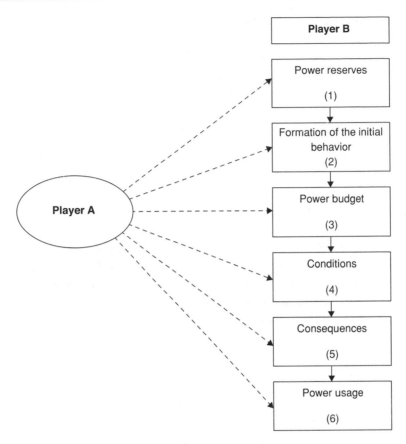

Figure 7.3   Influencing process of negotiating data

engagement (3), A again achieves a negative affect, since B is forced to distribute their powers in multiple fields, making them insufficient during the confrontation.

Affect efficiency: A is exercising a negative influence on B's conditions (4) – either the entire combination or just a specific type of condition – in order to reduce B's efficiency.

Concerning the entire combination, B seems to have insufficient technical conditions and therefore upgrades them within the entire mix of conditions, which reduces B's efficiency. Regarding specific types of condition, since B is effective in terms of legal conditions, A tries to delay matters and creates pressures to avoid any litigation in which B would probably win.

Shift the conflict behavior: namely:

(a) *Prevent* B's reactions by easing their conflict intensities.

(b) *Speed up* B's reactions by triggering significant intensities, leading them eventually to a conflict engagement.

(c) *Preserve* B's intensities by causing minor intensities that would force them to keep their powers on standby.

(d) *Delay or repress intensities* by limiting B's opportunities to express them.

(e) *Keep intensities under control* by counterbalancing B's deficits so that their intensities fall within A's acceptable consequences limit.

(f) *Force* B to cooperate by degrading their BATNA, in order that A's alternative for cooperation become more profitable for B.

(h) *Release* the relationship with B by improving B's BATNA.

(i) *Shift* B's interests by applying policies that would ultimately make their interests compatible with A's. Such policies represent *active interest-based bargaining*, given that the standard form of this negotiation's strategy is based on a passive acceptance of the other party's interests.

Let us follow some of these policies in case study 7.6:

Case study 7.6   Jenny risks losing her job because of Fred

Jenny, the 50-year old marketing manager of Electronics, risks losing her job because the new 35-year old sales manager, Fred, plans to control her subordinates in various ways and obtain control over the department's staffing. In his three years of employment with the company, he has managed to build up good relationships with members of the board of directors, whom he intends to exploit for his own purposes. Fred's intentions became obvious when Jenny – who has worked at Electronics for 20 years – confirmed, through third-party confidential information, that Fred intends to incorporate her department into his department.

1. If this incorporation came about, then Jenny would not accept having been downgraded, since she would lose standing in the eyes of her subordinates and her future dealings with them would be problematic. Consequently, her career in Electronics would come to an end.

2. Such a change would also cause trouble for the company, since Fred does not possess the essential knowledge that the sector requires and, thus, could not play a leadership role in client relationships.
3. Jenny's BATNA is the most unfavorable one because, at her age, she will find it difficult to obtain employment in a similar position or organizational level.
4. Conversely, Fred's BATNA is better, as he can easily apply for similar positions at similar organizational levels with other companies.

At this point, the main goal set by Jenny was to achieve a win–win resolution through interest-based bargaining. During discussions, Fred seemed to put her mind at rest, although his behavior remained the same. Furthermore, some of her subordinates, to whom it was clear that Fred was gaining more power over the entire department, started approaching him to ensure their future within Electronics. Jenny therefore understood that, so far, she had used an inappropriate strategy. Fred was heading towards a virtual negotiation without leaving her any alternative.

When she eventually began to seek allies that could help her deal with him, she found two groups. The first was represented by the managers of other departments who were concerned about Fred's growing power and close relationships with the members of the board. The second comprised her own employees, who were concerned they would be downgraded in the event that they were incorporated into the sales (Fred's) department.

What is worth stressing here is that Jenny was careful about not unveiling her tactics during her meetings with Fred. Instead of triggering conflicts, she was quite pliant, and also avoided being on the front-line when other people confronted him.

Three months later, Fred made the huge mistake everybody hoped he would. One of the company's major clients ceased dealing with the company, and another expressed his deep disappointment in Fred. The root of the problem was undoubtedly his arrogance and verbosity, but these had been cleverly worsened by the hidden tactics of the financial and production managers.

As a result, Fred began to lose confidence in the board's support and was close to quitting. In spite of the fact that Jenny could have taken considerable advantage of the situation, she did not push for his dismissal as she was well aware that his place could be taken by someone else just like him. In future, in order to allow her career to proceed smoothly until her retirement, her strategy would be to keep him in a weakened position and cause him multiple conflicts in various fields.

7.4 Isolated actions

There is sometimes the feeling that the parties do not intend to continue in a relationship or to deepen it. Instead, they have different ambitions (i.e. to obtain benefits from other sources). Even so, it is hard to discern whether an action that has been undertaken constitutes a virtual negotiation or an isolated ambition.

Let us take, for example, a conflict in which one party decides to file a suit against the other: is this a virtual negotiation or an isolated action? To answer the question, we need to know the exact intentions of the plaintiff. If they aim at changing the defendant's behavior (i.e. to obtain concessions or by blackmailing them), the lawsuit is considered a virtual negotiation. In the event that the plaintiff claims additional benefits – financial or emotional ones (i.e. to raise their income due to a large pay-out or to cause their opponent to be sent to a correctional institution) – then the action is isolated.

In this context, it is important to see how the two types are classified according to the BATNA. If the action is taken to improve the BATNA in order to increase negotiating power in an already-existing relationship, it represents the virtual process. Conversely, when improving the BATNA aims at ending a relationship, then it constitutes an isolated action. However, there are still cases where isolated actions do not intend to end but, rather, to complete a relationship. This cannot be classified as a virtual negotiation and will always cause indirect consequences (Example 7.5, p. 159).

Usually, isolated actions are the last option we would choose as the initial negotiating strategy. In other words, someone who adopts this kind of procedure has already tried other options, but to no avail. Case study 7.7 describes the path leading to an isolated action.

Example 7.6   Isolated actions

The employee is now certain that the employer cannot satisfy their request for a raise and, since he cannot improve his BATNA, he finds a second job to increase his income. Or he may even decide to start earning more money illegally from his primary job. However, these isolated actions affect his relationship with the employer because, if he finds a second job, he reduces his productivity level; if he begins earning more money illegally from his primary job, he causes the company shortfalls.

Case study 7.7   How Kate and Nick drifted apart

Kate, representative of Distillery, a large wine-producing company that also trades in the products of multinational corporations, wants to preserve the six-year relationship with Multinational, which is represented by Nick. Multinational is one of the largest companies in the sector, dealing with a broad range of international brand products. For each product category, Distillery is serviced by a different supplier.

1. Soon, the companies began to disagree about the price that Distillery had set to sell Multinational's products in the local market.
2. Distillery believed that selling Multinational's products at high prices can maximize their overall profit.
3. On the other hand, though, Multinational aimed mainly at increasing their market share through low prices.
4. Ultimately, Distillery managed to keep the prices high by convincing Multinational's representatives that Distillery would develop a special promotion strategy for high-priced, exclusive products.

During the first years, despite consumer complaints and complaints from Multinational about the high prices, sales increased significantly until they reached a standstill when the market's promotion resources began to decrease.

Up to that point there had seemed to be mere disagreement. The problem was exacerbated when Multinational changed the period in which Distillery was required to settle invoices. After a while, the problem became even worse when Distillery's competitors approached Multinational asking to retail their products (this would expand Multinational's negotiating power significantly). Thus, after several meetings Kate and Nick came up with a mutual solution: Distillery would agree to the shorter period in which to settle invoices, while Multinational would support the sale of its products in the local market with additional promotional programs.

No matter how hard the representatives tried to settle the issue, neither side kept to the arrangements – especially Multinational, who nationally stopped shipping products to Distillery branches until Distillery had settled all their invoices. As a result, the two companies ceased collaborating and, today, Multinational is being represented by another company.

Let us examine Kate and Nick's tactics during the negotiation period: Due to the initial agreement and the six-year relationship, they began with successful interest-based bargaining that relied on Nick's low "win" ambitions. In the course of the relationship, however, the interest of Distillery's competitors improved Multinational's BATNA. This multiplied Nick's "win" objectives so, as a result, he chose a virtual negotiation (i.e. he informed Kate that some Distillery competitors were quite interested in promoting Multinational's products).

Kate was unable to change the deadline for settling Multinational's invoices, since that would have obliged Distillery to settle with all its other suppliers within agreed time frames. In other words, the preservation of the cooperation between the two companies would bring Distillery a smaller profit than the value of the losses suffered in the event that they had to settle all suppliers' invoices promptly.

But what led to this outcome? Most probably, the main reason was the co-estimation of the *negative influences* and their *preservation*. Apart from that, the way Multinational pushed for a reduction in retail prices would cause a drastic drop in Distillery's profit. If Distillery accepted the change in policy, this decision would influence cooperation with any other companies – including Multinational.

This was the main reason why both parties proceeded with isolated actions which, although they caused the parties to drift apart, appeared to be the best possible solution in the circumstances.

7.5 Summary so far

In the previous sections, we determined the standard forms of handling conflicts through negotiations and their expanded variations.

Traditionally, negotiations presuppose the physical presence of the parties. However, the extension of negotiations to their *virtual* forms – and to isolated actions, which affect the outcomes of negotiations – multiplies the ways in which we can handle negotiations. This is because it allows the inclusion of a wider range of behaviors that, up to now, were considered purely as non-negotiating behaviors (e.g. interpersonal relationships, or other activities in the field of management such as marketing, supplies, finance, organizational relations, changes, leadership and so on).

After analysis of the ways of negotiating, it became obvious that there is no single way by which to achieve the anticipated outcome regardless of the circumstances. However, the anticipated outcome in every single case can be best achieved by choosing the most appropriation option from those available. The approach of this best-achieved outcome presupposes compatibility between our handling behavior and the details of each conflict episode, in the way described by our model.

Furthermore, regardless of the opportunities for planned adaptation, opportunities have been defined for interventions in the details at each stage in a conflict so as to shape them in such a way as to strengthen the planned methods of negotiation, or to orient them to our preferred methods where we have advantages.

7.6 Before the final decision

Before we decide on the negotiating methods that we are going to follow, we need to examine two further details:

- The combinations of the various negotiating behaviors.
- The possible reactions of the other party.

Negotiation behavior mix

The majority of examples have made it clear that the parties do not usually adopt just one negotiating strategy but, instead, refer to mixes or combinations of them.

Similar mixes are used by players to improve the level of their effectiveness, or to enable one player to introduce their preferences more smoothly into the other party's mix. As a rule, a mix comprises a priority choice (the basic preference) and secondary choices (those that support the main aim). However, telling the difference between the priority choice and the secondary choices is not always easy:

In this case, A's *main* choice is either the individual or collective agreement with C. Their *secondary* choice is engaging in a virtual process

---

Example 7.7   Negotiation behavior mix

Supplier A is negotiating directly with potential clients B and C. They are, however, mainly interested in signing an exclusive deal with C, because an exclusive deal with C offers greater financial opportunities. In the meantime, A also uses negotiations with B to improve their BATNA and maximize their negotiating power over C.

with C, since A is trying to increase C's insecurity by performing parallel negotiations with B.

Hence, in order to find out the most profitable mix, we use exactly the same method as when we need to choose the main negotiating behavior. There are four criteria that evaluate benefits and deficits:

- Cost or damages (power reserves).
- Profit (formation of the initial conflict behavior).
- Negative and positive influences (power budget).
- Duration of the influences (conditions).

Incongruous negotiating behaviors

If we take as a fact that each party chooses the negotiating behavior that maximizes their profit, then it might be that these are two entirely different negotiating behaviors. In order to distinguish the various mixes, we use Table 7.3.

The lines on Table 7.3 show the possible main negotiating behaviors of player A; the columns indicate the corresponding negotiating behaviors of

Table 7.3   Combined negotiating strategies among the parties

Player B:	Player A:	Direct negotiations		Virtual negotiations		Isolated actions
		Collective resolution (1)	Individual resolution (2)	Instead of the direct one (3)	Influencing the data (4)	Outside the relationship (5)
Direct negotiations	Collective resolution (1)	**1.1**	1.2	1.3	1.4	1.5
	Individual resolution (2)	2.1	**2.2**	2.3	2.4	2.5
Virtual negotiations	Instead of the direct one (3)	3.1	3.2	**3.3**	3.4	3.5
	Influencing the data (4)	4.1	4.2	4.3	**4.4**	4.5
Isolated actions	Outside the relationship (5)	5.1	5.2	5.3	5.4	**5.5**

player B. In other words, A is either going to choose a kind of direct or virtual negotiation, or move towards isolated actions. The same five options are also available to B and are presented in the columns of Table 7.3.

The total number of possible combinations of both A and B total 25. Of this number, only five – those inside the diagonal stripes – are congruous; the remaining 20 are totally incongruous. The five homogeneous negotiating behaviors are when both parties:

1. Prefer collective resolution.
2. Choose individual resolution.
3. Undertake virtual negotiation rather than direct negotiation.
4. Choose virtual negotiation, thus influencing the other party's data.
5. Try to achieve their goals outside their relationship.

Every other point on Table 7.3 shows options of negotiating behavior that are not homogeneous:

(1)–(4): A moves towards collective resolution (1), whereas B chooses virtual negotiation, thus influencing A's data (4).
(2)–(5): A chooses individual resolution (2), while B performs isolated actions (5).
(5)–(4): A chooses isolated actions (5), while B focuses on changing A's data.

Table 7.3 clearly demonstrates that the number of possible incongruous combinations is five times greater than the number of homogeneous ways to negotiate. This leads us to the reasonable conclusion that parties in conflict usually follow incongruous negotiating paths.

This conclusion is not yet supported through corresponding research However, I firmly believe that in most cases incongruence is the main feature of negotiating strategies. A glance at the way participants use corresponding combinations rather than just one negotiating strategy only supports my thesis. Given that there is such a variety of negotiating behaviors, there is a low likelihood that the combinations used by parties would match perfectly.

Is it possible to predict the other party's negotiating strategy? If so, what can be done to achieve that prediction? First, one should examine the benefits resulting from alternative behaviors by applying criteria that determine the consequences (i.e. the cost or damages, the profit, the positive and negative influences, and their duration). Hence, when the other party heads towards a behavior that would be unprofitable for our goals, we have the opportunity to intervene in their negotiating data, based on Figure 7.2, and consequently to shift the other party's behavior towards our interests.

This was the method that Stella and Vickie used successfully (case study 6.3(c), p. 137) when Kevin abandoned his initial plans. Jenny and Fred attempted the same in order to achieve interest-based bargaining (case study 7.6, p. 168). However, in Jenny's case, her efforts were non-productive because Fred thought that he could fulfill his objectives through virtual negotiation or isolated actions.

Concerning case study 7.6, I believe that Jenny could have easily predicted that collective resolution was never going to be achieved, since it would limit Fred's ambitions, which Fred would have no reason to do. Later in the conflict episode, Jenny adopted a negotiation strategy combination to which Fred could not respond.

I believe that, following this, Fred would prefer collective resolution with Jenny in the future. Jenny would reject this, since the negotiating combination she developed would have ensured her the long-term outcome she desired.

This entire analysis helps achieve a more dynamic consideration of negotiations. Thus, in a long-term view of matters, the players are no longer enclosed in a particular strategy or strategic mix. Instead, they have the possibility to evolve and develop means to suit their own needs as much as the other party's reactions.

It is no wonder, therefore, that taking such a complex structure comprised of numerous different outcomes and options into consideration is rather stressful. So, in order to avoid any stress whatsoever, it is advisable to rely on a solid framework (i.e. a relationship model: *atypical* or *typical*, and also compatible with the particular conflict behaviors of the parties).

The atypical model is based on corresponding relationships (informal agreements, dependencies, interdependencies and so on), or like the one chosen by Jenny when she engaged in a conflict with Fred (case study 7.6).

Jenny managed to trap Fred in a particular behavior, through the building of an alliance with third parties created to face him as a common adversary. If Fred had diverged from his set behavior, he would have to deal individually with each executive who had joined Jenny's alliance, or simply quit the field of conflict. The viability of this model was ultimately dependent on the ability of Jenny's supporters to preserve their benefits and the outcome of Fred's attempts to split the group.

On the other hand, the typical model includes typical, binding agreements, and is supported by special institutions (i.e. adjudication committees). This is the case where conflict management and negotiating outcomes become institutionalized.

Predicting and decoding behaviors

Regardless of any accurate planning or intelligent strategy, there is no definite way to succeed in a negotiation. The selected procedure might eventually prove to be inappropriate because of the other party's feedback. The adversary's response may cause unprofitable consequences in comparison with what had been initially planned. Hence, to facilitate any prediction of the other party's reaction, we use the procedure depicted in Figure 7.4, which shows every possible interaction between A and B.

Furthermore, Figure 7.4 is based on the concept that every party intends to distribute their powers effectively and profitably, thereby influencing the other party's data for the corresponding form of their behavior.

In other words, just as A may influence every aspect of B's behavior, B may influence A's behavior. At this point, it is important to highlight the

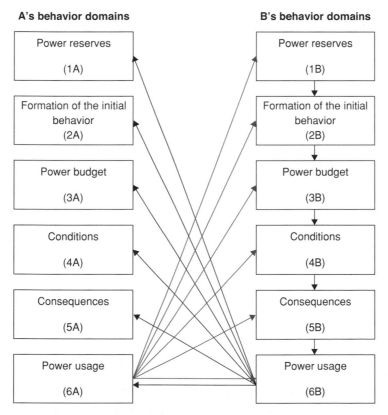

Figure 7.4 Interaction points between A and B's behavior

fact that each party's awareness of the repercussions that the adversary's actions may have on them leads inevitably to "self-restricting" policies.

That is why; A avoids inflicting damage on B if they consider that B can react in a similar way – at the same point, or at another point of equal significance – without having the ability to stop it. And when B steps outside the self-restricting framework, A restores B to their initial position by giving a reminder of the risk of causing major repercussions.

This is the very strategy that is used when new data enter a relationship; for example, B manages to disengage from certain fields and release the powers supporting those fields. Put simply: once the power reserves increase, B changes their power budget (3B) to invest against A and inflict greater damage.

What happens, then, if A is unable to worsen B's situation in some other field that could eventually absorb B's released powers? A should invest an equal amount of power to keep their conflict ability from decreasing.

This method can also be used for understanding B's tactics and manipulative actions.

Let us assume, for example, that B insists on a specific request that A cannot satisfy.

In this case, as soon as A evaluates the profit that B is going to obtain if they satisfy the request, they realize that it is disproportionately small when compared to B's insistence. So, six possible alternatives may arise:

1. B's request is just a pretext to push A in a difficult sector so as to make A ultimately proceed with concessions in some other sector in which B is interested.
2. B tries to counterbalance the shortfalls they experienced because of A by pushing them in a difficult sector.
3. B wishes to challenge A to a harsh reckoning, or intends to end their relationship.
4. B wants to satisfy their request to obtain benefits at another field of relationships in which A does not participate.
5. B acts on behalf of a third party against A.
6. Either A or B has miscalculated the real benefits B will gain if A satisfies B's request.

The conclusion that can be drawn is that the present method is of great help when it comes to developing and evaluating scenarios during the escalation of a conflict. When applied, it makes the choice of a negotiating behavior directly dependent on the other party's triggered consequences, given that each party has the ability to respond to the others' actions.

7.7 Reaching the end

Once the final decision is made, we eventually head towards the end of a conflict. A full depiction of a conflict's development is presented in Figure 7.5, which completes the series of figures presented in the previous units.

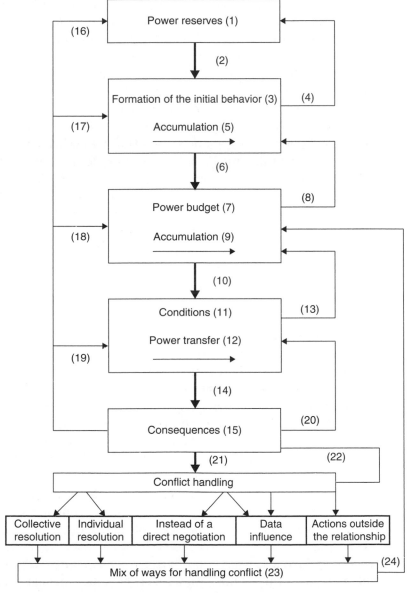

Figure 7.5 The course and end of the conflict episode

First, point (20) shows the decision to avoid engaging in the conflict (i.e. the decision not to use any power whatsoever when it becomes clear that the consequences are going to be harmful). At that point, we return to stage (11), where we examine the possibility of improving conditions in order to ensure the desired results when it comes to realizing our plans (14).

In the event that conditions cannot be improved, we go back to the previous stages, aiming at improving their data so as to return to the re-evaluation of consequences (14). Until that happens, the conflict stagnates in a state of accumulation (9).

Point (21) on the Figure 7.5 records the beginning of the negotiating behavior selection process, between the forms of direct negotiations, virtual negotiations, isolated actions, or a mix of them (23).

If the behavior becomes subject to change (22), then whether a party will adopt an alternative behavior presupposes the re-evaluation of consequences (16), (17), (18) and (19). In the event that the desired mix is difficult to find (23), the only available option is following the previous course of process re-evaluation (20).

Finally, the end of a conflict triggers influences (24) not only within the relationships between the participants, but also between third parties – even in irrelevant fields. Once there, in order to evaluate the influences, it is necessary to return to the power budget stage (7) and, in accordance with the data we analyzed, we may reach the final option.

7.8 Final remarks

In this chapter, we discussed two further topics that influence our decisions. The first refers to the mixes of *negotiating behaviors*. Traditionally, it is thought that each party chooses just one negotiating method, which can be alternated depending on their needs. However, everyday life shows that matters evolve quite differently: The players adopt just one behavior in simple cases; in more complex situations, they enrich their main choice with secondary options to create an efficient mix.

Hence, ignoring these mixes can only cause faulty evaluations. If, for example, the other party uses a mix of virtual negotiation and collective settlement but the other party is not aware of it, they may end up erroneously believing that the other party reacts based on collective resolution.

The second topic discussed in this chapter is *predicting and decoding the other party's behavior*. Often, we wonder about the other party's intentions or reactions to our behavior. The answers to these queries were based on the evidence of Figure 7.4, according to which each action undertaken by a player influences at least one aspect of the negotiating behavior of the other party. Thus, we are now able to see the adversary's purpose, putting us in a position to track down deceitful and disorienting actions.

Finally, even in the event of "peculiar" behaviors, it is easier to uncover the negotiating mixes and, ultimately, reduce the uncertainty regarding their actions and their behavior.

CHAPTER 8

Epilog

It is true that, in the real world, all negotiations are in touch with personal ambitions. They hinge on external developments; they are subjected to subversions because of imbalance in relationships and, of course, with crises. This often makes negotiations appear to be chaotic processes. However, as a "natural remedy" to this chaos we can follow two different paths.

The first path consists of ignoring the disorder, or trying to shrink it by developing a unique behavior model that maximizes our gain from all of our negotiations. Such a model is accepted as a panacea, since it may be applied to all kinds of situations – the most widely-known is that of Harvard's Program on Negotiation, which is built upon interest-based bargaining.

The second path accepts that negotiations may operate in complete disorder, and starts familiarizing us with the idea that there is no unique model covering all our needs. On the contrary, our behavior, as well as the model of negotiations we are going to use, should be adjusted to each unique case, and thus to adapt any possible changes of the negotiation data.

The approach that this book has attempted is oriented towards the second path, which builds its model upon the conflict-triggering motivation, from the very birth of it to the final stage.

So, in order to ensure reliability for the entire procedure, unquestionable relationship data were taken as the main starting point. This approach helped us realize that the various participants:

- Have limited power storage.
- Experience multiple parallel conflicts with many players, hoping to obtain different kinds of benefits.
- Do not display impulsive reactions (every strategy is carefully planned in advance).

At this point, it is necessary to underline that these data are not meant to question one's way of thinking or acting; in fact, they can fit any subjective reasoning perfectly, because even the unique way in which one perceives a power shortage, invests power on different conflicts, and plans reactions may be instrumental in interpreting their final behavior so as to make it predictable.

As a result, a similar approach is of great help, because it allows us to use quite flexible negotiating methods, does not bind us to just one cure-all model, and leaves room for one to adapt it to one's special needs. Therefore, the degree of reliability of our final choices depends on the relationship between the choices themselves and the conflict data (the conflict has already occurred and led to a negotiation).

In order to make a model fit chaotic conditions, it is advisable to maximize the benefit in every field of action and avoid focusing on just the isolated profit resulting from a particular negotiation. (This second scenario usually takes place when we have very few powers available, so we concentrate on a unique field of action, even if that means having reduced benefits). Thus, we are able to define the *boundaries of our engagement* – given that our behavior is *not the desired one but, rather, the one that allows us to be involved in more procedures.*

Moreover, if we examine this approach from an interpretative point of view, it becomes clear that it facilitates predicting the adversary's negotiating tactics and decoding their behavior. In addition to this, we have more opportunities to disengage from passive policies and, instead, develop active ones to influence the other party's final choices and behavior, depending on one's own ambitions. Finally, this strategy allows us to be prepared to change the data and eventually establish the desired negotiating model.

But how is it really possible to disengage? It is usually possible to disengage through the expansion of the negotiation towards more virtual forms and isolated actions that manage to influence the behavior of the participants.

According to the model, the two main objectives are:

- To interpret the final negotiating behavior.
- To understand each decision leading to the next process level.

Put simply: if we imagine the interconnected rings of a chain, we can understand why a player chose a particular conflict handling method by looking at the preceding stage of the consequences data, which depends on the preceding stage of consequences, which is based on conditions. The interpretation of the conditions stage itself begins at the power budget stage, which is based upon the data of the initial conflict behavior.

Hence, the model manages to render relationships in a wholly schematic way so as to have a behavior that is compatible with the negotiation mix and leads towards the desired outcome. Once this step is taken, it will be easier to answer whether the outcome of negotiations is more or less effective when:

- We hide our interest about a specific benefit, in order to avoid being pushed by the adversary at that point.
- We are aggressive, tough and determined.
- We invite many players to join the field of engagement.
- We bluff.
- We sit in front of or beside the other party.
- We cause the other party to feel insecure or uncertain.
- We trust the other party.
- We develop or we highlight any emotional relationship with the other party.
- We begin with the easy topics and then proceed to more unpleasant ones (or vice versa).
- We start a negotiation by saying "no."

Given that the answer to these questions may vary according to the negotiating model that has been chosen by the participants, it is better to co-estimate ambitions and activities in each field of conflict, together with the interactions between fields as well.

So, once the relationship data are determined, the players may begin a profitable negotiation by applying either the same or different negotiating models. If the existing model is useful, then the participants adapt their tactics to it; otherwise they influence its supporting data in order to establish a new one.

What has been exposed so far might provide the general guidelines to the decoding of common negotiating strategies. However, there is great potential in developing specialized models in fields such as business management, sales, marketing, human resources, industrial relations, public relations, strategy, organization, and planning, following a negotiating approach. The study of similar activities from a negotiating point of view can ultimately facilitate a pragmatic approach that today's lack of policy or idealized assumption that the parties "play with no adversary" has made it hard to attempt.

First, there is no conflict without the other party because every player aims at obtaining some profit – the entire conflict and the negotiating procedure are unquestionable.

In addition to this, the most serious consequence of the lack of politics is that, when there are obstacles, the only viable solution appears to be the re-consideration of objectives (see case study 1.1, p. 1). Once the approach has been made, there is a chance of dealing with any conflict or negotiation based on "political" behavior, such as that in Case 1.2 (p. 2).

Finally, the model analysis has so far avoided measuring or comparing powers, although the overall approach could provide statistical values based on the idea that comparing powers depends on the amount that players are allowed to invest effectively in all the other fields of relationships in order to gain the expected benefits.

bargaining 117, 147, 148, 149, 150, 153, 154, 155, 158, 159, 160, 161, 162, 168, 169, 172, 176, 182
BATNA 145, 153, 157, 158, 159, 160, 163, 165, 166, 168, 169, 170, 172, 173
behavior
   components 20, 38
   conflict 12, 13, 20, 82, 134, 166, 168, 174, 176, 183
   decoding 143, 177, 180, 183
   incompatible 17, 44, 46, 51, 61
   initial 17, 44, 51, 55, 83, 120, 122, 134, 135, 136, 137, 142, 177, 179
   negotiating 20, 37, 38, 45, 46, 56, 57, 88, 90, 101, 143, 144, 166, 172, 173,174, 175, 178, 180, 181, 183
   party 3, 5, 6, 16, 22, 33, 84, 116, 122, 125, 141, 142, 176, 180
benefit cost, cost of benefit 28, 46, 64
bluffing 25
boomerang effect 8

conditions
   ancillary 109, 110
   complementary 84, 91, 106, 108, 112, 113
   cultural 91, 99, 100, 101, 102, 106, 112, 113, 136
   expanding 114, 117
   favorable 111, 114, 118, 122
   financial 91, 92, 93, 102, 106, 110, 112, 113, 114, 116, 118
   legal 91, 101, 102, 103, 106, 112, 113, 115, 118, 119, 136, 167
   mix 84, 110, 114, 118, 119, 120, 167
   political 15, 91, 93, 94, 102, 106, 110, 112, 113, 114, 116, 118, 136, 139, 140
   prevailing 109, 111, 119
   profitable 111
   technical 91, 104, 105, 106, 110, 112, 113, 114, 118, 167
   time 91, 96, 97, 98, 102, 106, 111, 112, 113, 114, 119, 124
   unfavorable 111, 114

conflict
   ability 10, 11, 17, 20, 34, 35, 36, 37, 38, 39, 40, 41, 42, 43, 45, 46, 47, 48, 49, 50, 51, 53, 55, 56, 57, 67, 68, 69, 70, 71, 72, 73, 74, 75, 77, 78, 79, 82, 83, 134, 135, 139, 140, 152, 166, 178
   accumulation 18, 19, 20, 42, 49, 52, 57, 77
   action 18, 19, 42, 45, 49, 57, 73, 82
   control 24, 132
   depreciation 17, 18, 19, 20, 37, 38, 39, 40, 45, 46, 47, 49, 52, 57, 71
   efficiency 110
   emotional 22, 23, 24, 25, 26, 37, 73, 155
   field 4, 51, 53, 55, 56, 77, 83, 84, 96, 121, 135
   handling 6, 9, 33, 124, 125, 133, 143, 144, 179, 183
   of interest 4, 12
   management 176
   material 22, 23, 24, 29, 61, 73
   measurement 27, 32, 62
   model 8, 12
   parallel 4, 9, 10, 16, 53, 182
   resolution 152, 153; individual 143, 153, 158, 159, 162, 174, 175, 179;
     collective 143, 146, 148, 159, 160, 161, 174, 175, 176, 179, 180
   tension 140
consequences
   evaluation 12, 122, 160, 180
   negative 16, 129, 140
   sources 135, 136
cooperation
   degree of 30
   emotional 22, 23, 24, 25, 27, 29
   intensity 28, 30, 33
   material 22, 23, 24
criteria
   for determining consequences 125, 132
   priorities of 141

deficit cost, cost of deficit 28, 30
duration of influences 129, 130, 132, 137, 140

field
    components of 55
    conflict in 57
    flexible 79, 86
    inflexible 80, 86
    significance 66, 67, 73
    symbolic participation 53, 80, 81

isolated actions 143, 144, 170, 172, 174, 175, 176, 180, 183

negotiation
    direct 4, 6, 7, 143, 144, 146, 159, 161, 162, 163, 174, 175, 179, 180
    effective 7
    efficient 14,122
    realization of 12
    virtual 4, 6, 7, 143, 144, 162, 163, 166, 169, 170, 172, 174, 175, 176, 180

obstacles 1, 7, 91, 111, 112, 113, 114, 115, 116, 117, 118, 120, 163, 166, 185
    objective 2, 3
    subjective 3

passive
    acceptance 168
    adaptation 92

adjustments 16
behavior 123
policies 183
policies 95, 97, 113, 120, 129, 146, 164, 168, 178, 183
    active 92
    passive 183
politics 16, 185
    active 16
power
    budget 12, 13, 51, 52, 53, 54, 55, 82, 83, 88, 120, 122, 134, 135, 136, 137, 142, 166, 167, 174, 177, 178, 179, 180, 183
    distribution balance 34, 35
    excessive 14, 86, 87, 88
    insufficient 14, 46, 85, 119
    reserves 4, 9, 10, 11, 12, 14, 16, 17, 35, 36, 46, 51, 52, 53, 56, 68, 70, 73, 79, 80, 83, 84, 85, 86, 110, 116, 120, 122, 133, 134, 135, 136, 139, 142, 166, 167, 174, 177, 178, 179
    sufficient 10,11, 70, 81, 88, 116, 119

recipes 8, 12

synergy 81, 82, 114
    negative 114
    positive 81, 82, 114